THE ULTIMATE GIRLS' GUIDE TO PUBERTY

Everything You Need to Know About Your Changing Body, Mind, and Emotions as You Grow Up | A Girls Puberty Book for 8-12 year olds

AMANDA K. SMITH

ISBN : 9798861102414

CONTENTS

INTRODUCTION

☆ WELCOME AND WHY YOU SHOULD READ THIS BOOK

As you travel the path of growing up, one significant stop is the station of puberty. It might seem like a big word, even a little scary, but think of it as a roller coaster ride. Sure, it's filled with ups and downs, twists and turns, but in the end, it's sure to be an exhilarating adventure. An adventure that's all about you - your body, your mind, and your emotions.

First things first, what exactly is puberty? Simply put, puberty is a series of changes that your body goes through as you mature and get a step closer to becoming a young woman. It doesn't happen overnight, mind you! It's more like a space mission - exciting, a little bit mysterious, and one step at a time. Your body begins to produce hormones, nature's little way of telling your system that it's time to start this transformation. These hormones kickstart all sorts of changes in your body, from height and weight changes to the development of breasts and the beginning of menstruation. But, puberty isn't just about physical changes. Your brain and emotions are getting a makeover too as you navigate the world with a fresh perspective. Sometimes, you might feel like a bag of mixed emotions and that's perfectly fine. It's all a part of the growth!

Now, you might wonder why is this even happening? Why does your body suddenly decide to go through these drastic changes? Well, the answer lies within the magic of biology. Nature has designed our bodies to mature and reproduce once we reach a certain age, and puberty is that key moment when we transition from being kids to fertile young adults. Taking this journey of puberty is like turning the pages of an exciting new book – full of surprises, full of new growth, and full of self-discovery. However daunting it might seem, remember that this journey is a normal part of life, and every girl around the world goes through it. It's a badge of honor that says, "Hey, you're growing up!" While this journey might sometimes feel like a solo adventure, never forget that you're not alone. From parents and friends to teachers and trusted adults, there's always someone to turn to when the ride seems a little too bumpy. So buckle up, embrace the changes, learn about yourself, and most importantly, enjoy the ride.

From the sparkles in your eyes to the tips of your toes, so many amazing and exciting changes are underway as you embark on this journey of growing up. Our goal is to accompany you through all the twists and turns, ups and downs, joys and challenges you might face. Unexpected changes can sometimes be a bit unsettling, but when you have an understanding of what's happening, it becomes a bit easier to navigate. This is a handy source of trustworthy information that will provide answers to your questions. It is like a trusted big sister or a cool aunt who is ready to give you honest and helpful advice.

We'll help you understand:

☆ The physical transformations happening to your body, including growth spurts, hair growth, skin changes, and yes, the adventures of your period.

☆ The emotional roller coaster you might experience, which includes mood swings, feelings of insecurity, as well as excitement about the new world opening up in front of you.

☆ The changes in your brain that are sharpening your thinking, building your decision-making skills, and contributing to your unique personality.

★ And not to forget, we'll even touch upon the social changes you might notice around you, like shifting friendships, first crushes, and changing dynamics at home and in school.

Everyone's journey is different, and that's what makes each one of us special. This source is here to help you navigate your unique path with confidence and curiosity. Remember, all these changes mean you are growing up, and that's something to be celebrated! As you explore the pages, feel free to make notes, underline things, and write down any questions that come up. Knowledge is power, and you'll be amazed at just how strong, smart, and capable you are becoming. It's an honor to be by your side through this incredible journey, offering understanding and guidance.

Journal Exercise:

Reflect and write down three reasons why you wanted to read this book. Then, list out five things or topics you hope to learn from reading 'The Ultimate Girls' Guide to Puberty.' Feel free to express any fears, doubts, or questions you might have about this phase of your life. Keep in mind, it's okay not to know everything right now, the important thing is that you're taking steps to learn more.

☆ HOW TO USE THIS BOOK

So, you've got this book in your hands. "The Ultimate Girls' Guide to Puberty" is designed to be your personal guide, friend, and confidant as you navigate this unique and transformative phase of life called puberty. Let's go through how to get the most out of it!

I. Take It One Step at a Time:

This book is organized in a way that you can start from the beginning and move through each chapter sequentially, or you can jump to specific sections that you're most curious about. There's no right or wrong way to read it.

2. Use the Table of Contents:

Got a burning question about menstruation? Hop over to Chapter 3. Want to learn more about healthy habits? Chapter 6 is your go-to. The Table of Contents is your roadmap.

3. Make Notes:

Feel free to write in this book! Underline the parts that resonate with you, jot down questions or thoughts in the margins, or even use sticky notes. This is your personal journey, and making notes can help you reflect and remember.

4. Take Breaks:

Some of this information might be a lot to process, and that's okay. Take breaks when you need, come back when you're ready.

5. It's Okay to Share:

While this is your personal guide, you might find it helpful to share some parts with a trusted adult or friend, especially if you have questions or need more understanding.

6. Dive into the Resources:

At the end of the book, there's a 'Resources and Support' section. Here, you'll find additional books, websites, helplines, and support groups that can offer more information or help.

7. Remember, It's All Normal:

You might come across information that makes you go, "Is this normal?" Yes, it is! Everyone's experience with puberty is unique, but the feelings, changes, and challenges you'll read about are all a typical part of growing up.

8. Revisit Often:

As you grow and change, you might find different sections of the book more relevant. It's a guide you can come back to again and again, anytime you need.

9. Keep an Open Mind:

Some chapters might be more relevant to you right now, while others might be for future you. Keep an open mind and absorb what feels right for your current stage.

10. Trust Yourself:

While this book provides a lot of information, always trust your instincts and feelings. You know yourself best.

Finally, remember that while this book is a great resource, it's just one tool in your toolkit. Always feel free to seek out trusted adults, friends, or professionals to chat about what you're experiencing or feeling. Enjoy the journey, embrace the changes, and remember: puberty is a natural part of growing up. You got this!

WHAT IS PUBERTY, ANYWAY?

☆ UNDERSTANDING PUBERTY

Hello there, young explorer! As you journey into this new phase of life, you might hear the word 'puberty' quite a lot. But what does it really mean? Let's dive in!

What is Puberty?

In simple terms, puberty is the time in your life when your body starts to change from that of a child to that of an adult. It's a phase when your body gears up to be able to reproduce one day. It's like when a caterpillar transforms into a butterfly; it's nature's way of preparing you for the next stage of life.

Why Does Puberty Happen?

Our bodies are amazing, aren't they? Underneath our skin, there's a complex system at work, powered by *hormones*. These are like little messengers that tell different parts of our bodies when and how to change. When you reach a certain age, your brain sends a signal to release these hormones, kickstarting the puberty process.

The Physical and Emotional Ride

During puberty, you'll notice both physical and emotional changes. Physically, you might grow taller, develop breasts, get your period, and see hair growing in new places. Emotionally, you might feel mood swings, become more self-conscious, or even develop crushes. Remember, all these changes are a natural part of growing up.

Everyone's Timeline is Different

Just as we all have unique fingerprints, our puberty journey is unique too. Some might start these changes as early as 8, while others might begin around 12 or later. It's all okay. Your body knows what it's doing and will work at its own pace.

Boys Go Through It Too!

While this book is tailored for girls, it's good to know that boys go through puberty as well. Their changes are a bit different (like their voices deepening and shoulders broadening), but the emotions and the uncertainty can be pretty similar.

In Conclusion

Think of puberty as an adventure — it's a time of discovery, growth, and understanding more about who you are. Just like any adventure, there might be moments of excitement, moments of uncertainty, and moments that leave you with a ton of questions. And guess what? That's what this book (and trusted adults in your life) is here for! So buckle up and get ready for this incredible journey called puberty.

☆ 1.2 TIMELINE: WHAT TO EXPECT WHEN

Now that you've got an idea of what puberty is, you might be wondering about the specifics. When will certain changes happen? What order do they come in? While everyone's experience can differ slightly, there's a general timeline that many people follow. Let's break it down!

Early Changes (Around 8-11 years old)

Growth Spurt: One of the first signs is often a growth spurt. You might notice your clothes getting a bit tight or your shoes feeling small. This is your body starting to stretch out.

Breast Buds: Tiny, tender lumps might form under one or both nipples. These are called breast buds, signaling the start of breast development.

Body Hair: Fine, light hair might start appearing on your legs, under your arms, or around your private parts.

Middle Changes (Around 11-14 years old)

Menstruation: This is a big one! Most girls get their first period during these years. But don't worry, we've got a whole chapter dedicated to this topic later on.

Breasts: They'll continue to grow and take on a more rounded shape.

Pubic Hair: The hair around your private parts will become thicker, curlier, and darker.

Oily Skin and Acne: Hormones can make your skin oilier, which sometimes leads to pimples or acne.

Later Changes (Around 14-18 years old)

Final Growth: By the end of this phase, most girls have reached their adult height, although some might continue to grow a little more.

Hips Widen: You might notice your hips getting a bit broader.

Regular Menstrual Cycle: While your early periods might be unpredictable, they typically become more regular over time.

Emotional Changes (Throughout Puberty)

Throughout all these physical changes, you'll likely experience a rollercoaster of emotions. One moment you might feel on top of the world, and the next, you might feel down or frustrated. These feelings are all valid and are a natural part of puberty.

Remember...

It's Okay to Be Early or Late: Everyone's body has its own schedule. If you're one of the first among your friends to see changes or one of the last, that's perfectly okay.

Your Experience is Unique: Just because your best friend or cousin went through something at a certain age doesn't mean you will too. Embrace your journey.

It's Not Just About the Body: Puberty is a time of mental and emotional growth too. It's all part of becoming the amazing adult you're meant to be!

Stay curious and patient. This is a time of transformation, and just like any transformation, it takes time. We're here with you every step of the way!

AGE RANGE	PHYSICAL CHANGES
8-10 years	Growth spurt
10-12 years	Pubic hair growth
12-14 years	Breast development
14-16 years	Menstruation becomes regular
16-18 years	Breast and body hair growth complete

Journal Exercise:

Reflect on the chapter you've just read: 'Timeline: What to Expect When'. Now, try to put yourself in the timeline of puberty.

1. Write down three physical changes that you have learned about and what you feel about them. Are there any ones you are excited about or apprehensive about, and why?

2. How does your understanding of puberty compare to what you thought before reading this chapter? Write about any misconceptions you had and how they may have changed.

3. Think about the emotional changes that happen during puberty. How might you handle these changes? What are some techniques you could use?

Remember, this is your personal journey, there is no right or wrong answer. These changes are a normal part of growing up and everyone experiences them differently.

☆ 1.3 PUBERTY IS DIFFERENT FOR EVERYONE

Puberty is a unique journey for every girl. Each one of us is different and that's what makes us special! Just like no two snowflakes are the same, no two girls go through puberty in exactly the same way or at the same time. Let's delve into this topic and understand how these differences can be recognized and embraced. Your body is a fantastic piece of art, which follows the rhythm of nature. Around ages 8-12 years, many girls start experiencing changes in their bodies. You may notice grown-ups saying "You're blossoming into a young woman", which indeed, is true! While this transformation might seem a little mysterious and perhaps even scary at first, it's important to remember that it's a totally natural part of growing up. The physical changes you notice might include, your height increasing, weight fluctuating, or your breasts beginning to develop. Some girls might even get their first period, commonly known as menstruation. It's fascinating how your body works, right?

Remember, change is unpredictable and it doesn't follow a set pattern. It can happen gradually, or all at once. A friend might grow taller than you almost overnight, while some may still be waiting for their growth spurt. It's not a race, we all grow at our own pace, and that's perfectly fine! Rest assured, all these changes are a sign that your body is building a path towards becoming a woman. Embrace each change, understand that there can be variations in experiences. It is normal to feel different from friends or peers since we're all on our own unique journeys. Comparisons are almost inevitable as girls go through puberty. While it's natural, try not to compare yourself to others too much. We can't control when the changes will happen, and they might not commence at the same time for everyone. By all means, it's okay to want answers or reassurance. Talk openly to those around you who you trust - your mom, sister, aunt, teacher, or a doctor. They've been through similar experiences and would be glad to assist.

Let's summarize the key understanding points about individual differences in puberty:

★ Each girl experiences puberty differently.

★ Changes can take place gradually or all at once.

★ Comparisons with others are common, but remember that everyone's puberty timeline is unique.

★ It's beneficial to talk about your feelings and experiences with those you trust.

Now that you understand the individual differences that occur during puberty, it's easier to accept these changes patiently and gracefully. Remember, there's no need to rush or worry. Your body is doing exactly what it needs to do at its own pace, which is the perfect pace for you. In the next section, you'll learn even more about embracing the changes that come with puberty. For example, understanding the emotions that might surprise you, and appreciating the ever-evolving you. So, let's continue this exciting journey of discovery together! Don't worry, there's a lot of fun waiting for us on the other side.

Just when you thought dealing with the physical changes was enough, here come the emotions. One minute you're laughing with your friends and the next, you're irrationally annoyed. And guess what? That's perfectly normal! Puberty isn't just about your body, it's also about your feelings and thoughts. So, let's uncover those emotional changes one by one. First things first, your brain is developing during puberty, especially a part called the "Amygdala". This is the region responsible for emotions, so you might feel like you're on an emotional roller coaster. One moment happy, the next moment sad. You might cry at things you never used to find sad, or get angry quicker than you used to. This is due to the surge of hormones in your body, mainly estrogen and progesterone.

Secondly, you might start feeling self-conscious. Your body is changing, and so is your appearance. It's normal to have moments when you feel insecure, embarrassed, or even anxious about the way you look. Just remember, everyone your age is going through similar feelings and changes. Stay positive and remind yourself that these changes are a natural part of growing up. Next, you might notice an increase in mood swings. One minute you're on top of the world, and the next you're feeling extremely sensitive. This is quite common during puberty because of the fluctuating hormone levels. When you feel overwhelmed, take a few deep breaths, do a fun activity, or just take a little time for yourself. Keep in mind that it's important to express your feelings. It's perfectly alright to have strong emotions, but it's also essential to learn how to manage them. Never hesitate to talk to a trusted adult if you're finding it tough to handle these intense feelings. Lastly, it's pretty normal to argue more with your parents or friends during this stage because you're trying to establish your identity. You're growing up and your perspectives on certain things might change.

Dealing with these emotional changes can be challenging. Here are a few tips for navigating them:

★ Practice good self-care techniques like regular exercise, adequate sleep, and balanced meals. These can help you maintain a positive mood and reduce crankiness.

★ Take a ‚time out' when you feel your emotions escalating. This could be listening to music, reading, or just taking a few deep breaths.

★ Keep a journal to jot down your feelings. This can help you make sense of your emotions and understand what triggers your moods.

★ Be patient with yourself. Allow yourself to feel these emotions without beating yourself up about it.

★ Talk to someone when you're feeling overwhelmed. This could be a parent, teacher, school counselor, or a good friend. You're not alone in this journey and there are people willing to help and support you.

The emotional changes of puberty can be a wild ride, but remember that it's a journey everyone goes through. Accepting these changes and learning to manage them, is all part of the growing up process.

Journal Exercise:

Take a moment to think about the different changes you've heard about or noticed in yourself or around you.

1. List down the physical changes that you noticed first. How did that make you feel?

2. Write about any emotional changes you've been going through. How are these changes affecting your daily life?

3. Do you know of any friends who are experiencing puberty differently than you? Record about their experiences and reflect on how it makes you feel.

4. Draw yourself today. After a couple of months, draw yourself again, noticing any changes.

5. Finally, write a letter to your future self, expressing your feelings about going through these changes.

Remember, everyone is different and it's completely okay to feel confused, excited, or scared. Your feelings are valid. Take your time and remember this is your personal space to express yourself. There are no right or wrong answers, only reflections of your journey.

ALL ABOUT YOUR BODY

☆ 2.1 PHYSICAL CHANGES: THE BASICS

Get ready, because your body is about to go on one incredible journey! It's just as exciting as all those thrilling tales you've read or heard about, except this time, it's happening in real life. Let's dive in and explore these mysteries. Think of your body as an artist's canvas. The artist is your DNA, inherited from your mom and dad. At this stage, the picture starts to change and the beautiful masterpiece that is the grown-up you begins to take shape. The showstopper of this transformation is usually breasts. One day you may just start to notice them feeling a bit sore and starting to grow. This is normal. Each girl develops at her own pace, so don't worry if your best friend is ahead of you or even behind you. Another major change will be the growth of pubic hair. Just like your tummy gets bigger as you grow, your body starts to add some new patterns. The hair, commonly curly and coarse, usually starts appearing in a small area and gradually fills in over the course of a few years. You know how superheroes wear capes? Imagine your skin is like your very own superhero cape! But during puberty, your skin, especially on the face, might become oilier which may lead to acne or pimples. This is result of your oil glands becoming more active, another perfectly normal part of growing up.

Now, let's talk about the big stuff - periods. A period is when blood is released from your body through the vagina. It's part of the process that prepares your body for the possibility of pregnancy. This usually happens once a month from around the age of 11-14, but it might be earlier or later for some girls. And finally, you might start noticing a sudden growth spurt—almost as if someone zapped you with a magic growing stick while you were asleep. Again, it's just your body's unique timeline of transforming you into the amazing young lady you're becoming. These changes may seem a bit confusing and frustrating sometimes, but remember, they're what make you special, unique, and ultimately, a young woman.

PHYSICAL CHANGE	WHAT IT MEANS	HOW TO DEAL WITH IT
Growth Spurts	Sudden increase in height and weight	Eat healthy & sleep well
Breast Development	Starting of breast buds	Invest in a good sports or training bras
Body Hair	Hair growing in pubic area and underarms	Maintain good hygiene habits
Menstruation	Beginning of monthly periods	Use sanitary products & track your cycle
Skin Changes	Possible occurrence of acne	Maintain a clean skin routine

Puberty can feel like a rollercoaster, but don't worry, you're not alone! Everyone has questions, fears, and worries during this time. Remember to talk to someone you trust about your feelings - it can be a parent, an older sibling, a teacher, or a friend. Breaking the silence and sharing your thoughts can make all the difference. Embrace these changes as a part of your journey towards becoming an amazing young lady. Remember, you are unique, and your body is too! So go ahead, navigate these milestones with confidence, patience, and curiosity.

Journal Exercise:

1. What are some of the physical changes we talked about in this chapter? List them.

2. How do you feel about going through these changes? Write down your thoughts and emotions.

3. Identify three positive attributes about these physical changes. Why are they good?

4. Do you have any worries or questions about these physical changes? Write them down.

5. Imagine you are talking to a friend about these changes. What advice would you give her based on what you have just learned?

☆ 2.2 YOUR REPRODUCTIVE SYSTEM

In your journey of growing up, your body undergoes many changes. One of them includes the development of your reproductive system, a complex network of organs and structures designed for the purpose of reproduction. A basic understanding of your own anatomy provides a solid groundwork for the changes you will experience during puberty. At the heart of the female reproductive system are the **ovaries**. These are small, almond-shaped organs located in your lower abdomen on either side of your uterus. Each ovary holds numerous potential eggs, or ova. As you start puberty, your ovaries will begin releasing mature eggs during a monthly cycle known as menstruation.

The **uterus**, often called the womb, is a pear-shaped organ where a baby will grow if an egg is fertilized. Its strong, muscular walls stretch during pregnancy to accommodate the baby. However, if the egg is not fertilized, the lining of the uterus, called the "endometrium", is shed during menstruation.

The **fallopian tubes** are thin tubes that are attached to the upper part of the uterus and serve as tunnels for the egg cells to travel from the ovaries to the uterus. Conception, the fertilization of an egg by a sperm, usually happens in the fallopian tubes.

The **cervix** is the lower part of the uterus opening into the vagina. It's like a canal that allows menstrual blood to exit the uterus, and sperm to enter during sexual intercourse. During childbirth, the cervix expands to allow the baby to pass into the birth canal.

The **vagina**, also known as the birth canal, is a flexible tube that connects the cervix and the vulva. It's where menstrual blood leaves the body from the uterus and is also where a baby is delivered.

The **vulva** is the external part of the female genitalia. It includes the labia, the clitoris, and the vaginal opening. Each part of the vulva has a different role, from protecting your reproductive organs to sexual sensitivity.

It's normal to have questions or feel curious about your own anatomy. Remember, it's designed to do incredible things - from giving life to allowing you to experience new sensations and emotions as you grow up. For now, your body is preparing you for all these amazing changes and possibilities!

Now that understanding your anatomy is out of the way, it's time to unravel the mysteries of menstrual cycle and its nuances. Understand that each cycle is a narrative of potential reproduction, preparing your body for a possible pregnancy. Time to take you to the next part of the journey: The hormonal orchestra – understanding the menstrual cycle and hormonal changes. While it might seem a little mysterious, understanding the menstrual cycle and why it's important is actually quite straightforward, and there's no need for it to feel like a daunting topic.

The menstrual cycle usually begins between ages 8 and 16, marking the start of your body's journey toward womanhood. Your body starts making different hormones which signal your ovaries to produce eggs. This is called ovulation. If an egg isn't fertilized by sperm within about a day of being released, it will dissolve, and the lining of your uterus, which thickened in anticipation of a possible pregnancy, will shed. That's where your period comes in. A period, also known as menstruation, is the monthly process in which the body gets rid of these tissues and an unused egg.

★ Your periods usually starts as a light flow for a couple of days which gradually becomes heavier for a few more days and then slows down.

★ You can expect your first period to be a little lighter than future periods, and it might also be irregular for a few years as your body adjusts to all of these changes.

★ Periods usually last between 3 to 8 days. It varies from girl to girl and may change the length of time or the flow intensity as you grow up.

★ On average, you'll get your period every 21 to 35 days.

Now, let's talk about why the menstrual cycle is important. Understanding your menstrual cycle and recognizing the signs of your periods can help you feel more in control of your body. Being aware of the changes that you might experience can help you better prepare for them. Besides, tracking your cycle helps you understand your unique patterns and anticipate your next period. You'll know better when to carry around an extra pad or tampon, or when you might need some extra self-care. This information can also be very helpful as it serves as a marker for your reproductive health. When you're older, if your periods are regular, this indicates that your hormones are balanced and that the rest of your body is healthy, too. So, let's remember, growing up and going through these changes is perfectly normal—it's a natural part of becoming a young woman. This transformation is truly a thing of wonder, and it's something worth understanding and celebrating.

PART OF THE SYSTEM	FUNCTIONS	SIGNS OF MATURATION
Ovaries	Production of eggs and hormones	First period (menarche)
Uterus	Houses and nourishes developing fetus	Growth and widening of the hips
Vagina	Connects uterus to external body	Passage for menstruation and childbirth
Breasts	Produce milk for breastfeeding	Breast development and tenderness
Endocrine System	Regulates hormone production	Hormonal acne

Journal Exercise:

1. What are three interesting facts you learned about your reproductive system in this chapter?

2. How did you feel while reading about your reproductive system? Why do you think you felt this way?

3. Imagine that you have to explain the reproductive system to a younger friend or sibling - how would you explain it to them in simple terms?

4. Make a list of any questions or concerns you have about your reproductive system after reading this chapter.

5. Draw a small picture or write a poem or a paragraph that captures something about the reproductive system that you find fascinating.

☆ 2.3 BREAST DEVELOPMENT

Breasts, you might have heard of them, seen them, and perhaps even have small ones already, or not yet. No worries! They're indeed a significant part of our biological growth. Everyone girl's journey is unique, and it's crucial to understand that these changes take place at a different pace for everyone. Breast development marks the commencement of puberty in girls. It is a sign that our bodies are maturing and preparing for future possibilities like having babies. This exciting journey is called 'Thelarche.' Scientifically, it all begins when the brain sends signals to the ovaries, leading to the production of a hormone called estrogen. Estrogen is the true mastermind behind breast growth. It signals the fatty tissue in the chest area to start enlarging, and it also stimulates the dark area around the nipple, known as the areola, to expand. As the fatty tissues grow, that's when you notice the first subtle swellings - the beginning signs of budding breasts!

Just beneath the areola, milk ducts are beginning to develop. In case you're wondering -no, you're not preparing for making milk right now! These changes are an early preparation for potential future adventures of motherhood. During this stage you might notice that the chest area can be tender or mildly painful, which is quite normal. The pace of growth is different for everybody. Some may observe notable changes within a few months, for others, it may take a few years. But rest assured, it's all part of the big beautiful plan of puberty. Moreover, you might see one of your breasts growing faster than the other. That's perfectly fine. Most people have one breast slightly larger than the other.

It's important to remember that everyone's breasts are unique. The size, shape, and color can vary considerably from person to person, even within the same family! When you compare yourself with others, keep this in mind, and embrace your unique self. Puberty is not a race! Overall, the process of breast development is a fascinating dance of hormones, glands, and tissues. You're witnessing the miraculous workings of your own body. Nourish and care for it. Amid all these changes, take care of your emotional health as well, because you are more than all these physical changes. You are growing up, and it's an amazing journey of transformation and self-discovery. The story of who you're becoming is still being written, and you are the one holding the pen.

STAGE	WHAT TO EXPECT	DURATION
Stage 1	Pre-puberty	no changes yet
Stage 2	Breast buds grow	areolas darken
Stage 3	Breasts and areolas continue to expand	11-12 years

STAGE	WHAT TO EXPECT	DURATION
Stage 4	Areolas and nipples form separate mounds	13-14 years
Stage 5	Breasts reach final adult size	15+ years

When you begin to notice changes in your body, especially in your breasts, it is perfectly normal to feel a whirlwind of emotions. Sometimes, these changes can be exciting, other times, they might feel a tad confusing, or even overwhelming. And that's okay. All girls go through this, you are not alone. Here are some tips to keep your self-image and confidence intact as you navigate this part of your life. First, understand that everyone is unique. Your body is changing according to its own unique time table and that's perfectly fine. Some girls start puberty earlier or later than others, and breast development can be different for everyone. The size, shape, and rate of development of your breasts are all determined by your own unique biology and genetics. So, don't compare yourself with others. Embrace your own individual growth and development journey. Remember the importance of comfort and support. As your breasts begin to grow, they might feel tender or sensitive. A soft, comfortable bra or a training bra can provide needed support. You may also want to begin shopping for bras or training bras - it can be a fun and self-affirming experience. Plus, investing in a well-fitted bra can help you to feel more comfortable and confident as your body changes.

Stay active. When we exercise, our bodies produce endorphins - these are 'feel good' hormones that help boost our mood. Regularly participating in physical activities you enjoy can be a great way to maintain positive feelings towards your changing body. Also, sports and exercise keep you fit and healthy and remind you of the amazing things your body can do. Practice self-care and self-love. This includes physical self-care, like eating nutritious food, getting enough sleep and maintaining good hygiene. But remember, looking after your emotions is also a crucial part of self-care. Take some time out each day to relax, do something you enjoy and appreciate your body for the amazing changes it's going through. Lastly, talk about it. Don't bottle up your feelings or thoughts. Chat with someone you trust, a mother, an older sister or a friend who has gone through the same changes. It can be really helpful to share your experiences and feelings, and to hear from others who've been in the same situation. Remember that it's completely okay to have complex feelings about your changing body - there are people around you who would want to hear about it and help.

Remember, puberty is a normal and natural process, and each girl's journey is unique. It's an exciting time of change and growth, and it's okay to have mixed feelings about it. Always be patient with yourself, and treat your body with the kindness and respect it deserves. You're growing up, and that's something to be celebrated. Dealing with change isn't always easy, but with the right mindset, and emotional well-being, you can navigate through this phase confidently. Puberty is an integral part of your life journey and these changes, though sometimes strange, are just your body's way of preparing for adulthood. So, celebrate each step and remember, you're not alone. Every girl experiences these changes, and you're just as beautiful and amazing as you've always been. Remember that confidence comes from within. Believe in yourself, be proud of who you are, and of the amazing person you're becoming. With time and patience, you'll navigate through these changes smoothly.

Journal Exercise:

Take a few quiet moments to reflect on your reading. How are you feeling about the changes your body is going through? Are there any questions or uncertainties that popped up while reading the chapter on breast development?

1. Write down three things you learned about breast development. Try to describe in your own words how this is a normal part of growing up.

2. Do you feel comfortable or uncomfortable with these changes, or a bit of both? Explain why.

3. How can having more knowledge about this topic help you feel more comfortable with your own body development?

4. Think about how you can support your best friend if she starts going through these changes before or after you do. Write down three things you would say or do.

Remember, every girl's puberty journey is unique and that's what makes us special. Reminder, it's okay to talk to trusted adults about your feelings and questions. They've gone through it too!

☆ 2.4 BODY HAIR AND SKINCARE

That tingling sensation you're feeling right now? It's nothing but your body's way of saying, "Surprise! I'm changing." Believe it or not, one of these surprising changes you will soon notice is the growth of body hair. Hair will sprout in places you weren't expecting and might even feel a little strange at first, but trust me, it's all perfectly normal and part of growing up. Hair growth is an important stage of puberty, and something that every girl experiences. It starts to show up in different areas of your body, and at different times. This new hair signifies that your body is starting to mature. Fun fact: Body hair is actually meant to protect and warm our bodies. Our ancient ancestors were covered in a lot more hair than we have today.

You might be wondering why you don't see adults walking around covered in hair like a woolly mammoth. That's because, over time, as humans evolved, we lost most of our body hair. But a trace of it remains in each one of us, waiting to make its debut during puberty. The funny thing about body hair is that it doesn't grow in all at once, but in stages. The first place you might notice this new hair is under your arms. This usually happens between the ages of 9 and 14. Right around the same time or shortly after, you may start to observe hair growing in the pubic area. Don't be alarmed - it's completely normal. This hair usually begins as thin and light but gradually becomes thicker and darker as you grow older. Next on the list might be your legs, and even arms. You may notice your leg and arm hair becoming darker and more noticeable. But remember, everyone is different. Some girls may end up with a lot of hair on their legs and arms, while others may have very little. It all depends on your genetics - thank you, Mom and Dad!

Can you guess where the other surprising location new hair might start appearing is? Well, here's a clue. You've got two of them and you use them to eat corn on the cob. That's right - your upper lip! Don't worry, it's perfectly natural to notice a bit of hair above your lip. Most of the time they're very fine and hardly noticeable, unless you're looking for them. I know what you're thinking – why would nature play such a hairy trick on girls? But bear in mind, these changes are all a normal part of growing up. And guess what, boys go through them too, sometimes even more radically!

So, the big question is - what to do about this hair? Some girls feel perfectly comfortable with their new body hair, while others might feel self-conscious. And that's okay! If you decide you want to remove some of your body hair, there are several safe methods to do so, like shaving or waxing. But always remember to ask for an adult's help first. The most important thing to remember, as you journey through puberty and face all these changes, including growing body hair, is that it's all part of becoming the amazing woman you're destined to be. Embrace these changes. Remember, you're not alone in this journey - everyone goes through it. Be patient, celebrate your body's journey, and remember that this is just a small chapter in the exciting story of your life.

As your body matures, you might start to notice some changes in your skin. This can include everything from oily patches to unwelcome spots. These changes are brought about by the very same hormones that are guiding you towards adulthood. Understand that every girl goes through this process; after all, it's a sign of growing up. But don't worry, there are plenty of ways you can manage acne, blemishes, and keep your skin glowing. First things first: Hydration. Drinking lots of water helps keep your skin moisturized from the inside out. Aim for at least eight glasses a day. Water flushes out toxins from your body; they could potentially show up on your skin if you're not hydrated enough.

Next up: Cleanliness. Regular washing can support your skin health. Try not to overdo it though. Washing your face too frequently can strip it of its natural oils, leading it to produce even more oiliness if not done properly. So, aim to cleanse your face twice a day - morning and before going to bed. A simple skincare routine can work wonders as well. A gentle cleanser is a good start. In the morning, follow it up with a moisturizer that contains sunscreen. At night, after cleansing, opt for an oil-free moisturizer.

Acne is pretty normal, especially during puberty. The hormone fluctuations can trigger an excess production of oils in your skin. These oils, along with dead skin cells, can clog your pores, leading to spots or acne. But don't fret - there are ways to manage it. Over-the-counter acne treatments can be helpful. Look for products that contain salicylic acid or benzoyl peroxide. These ingredients can help clear up acne by unclogging pores and reducing inflammation. Always follow the instructions on the package, and if your skin starts feeling too dry or irritated, cut back on usage. It's tempting to squeeze a pesky pimple, but resist the urge! Picking, popping, or squeezing can cause more inflammation, increase the risk of scarring, and delay healing. Instead, try a spot treatment and let it do its magic.

Another crucial element is your diet. Eating a balanced diet with lots of fruits and vegetables can give your skin the nutrients it needs to stay healthy. On the other hand, foods high in sugar can trigger breakouts. So, balance them out with food rich in vitamins A, C, and E. Remember, everyone's skin is different. What works for your friends might not work for you. So, it's about figuring out what your skin needs and sticking with it. Whether that's more hydration, gentler products, or dietary changes. Finally, be patient. Skin changes during puberty are temporary. Your skin's oil production should settle back down as your hormones level out. Keep up with a consistent skincare routine, and make sure to love your skin in all its unique, changing glory! Maintain good skincare habits, always wear sunscreen, hydrate yourself, eat a balanced diet, and remember to be patient. Growing up is a journey, and your skin is part of that beautiful process. Your glowing skin is just around the corner. So, hang in there, and remember, if you ever have struggles with your skin, it's completely ok to reach out for help from a dermatologist. Beautiful skin happens with consistent effort and the right knowledge.

BODY PART	CHANGES DURING PUBERTY	SKINCARE TIPS
Armpits	Hair begins to grow	Use a gentle fragrance-free deodorant
Legs	Hair becomes more noticeable	Moisturize regularly to prevent dry skin

BODY PART	CHANGES DURING PUBERTY	SKINCARE TIPS
Face	Oil production might increase causing acne	Wash face twice daily with a mild cleanser
Chest	Some hair might appear around nipples	Use a gentle body wash for sensitive skin
Pubic Area	Hair begins to grow	Keep the area clean and dry
Back	Oil production might increase causing acne	Wash regularly with a non-comedogenic body wash

Journal Exercise:

1. Write down three changes you noticed about your body hair or skin recently.

2. How do you feel about these changes? Are there any that make you uncomfortable?

3. Research one method to take care of your skin or manage your body hair. Describe why you think it may or may not work for you.

4. Draw a picture of you trying this new method. Remember, it's okay if you aren't an artist, the important thing is to express yourself.

5. Imagine that your friend is feeling insecure about the changes she is going through with her body hair and skincare. Write an encouraging letter to her reminding her that change is a part of growing up.

☆ 2.5 HEIGHT, WEIGHT, AND BODY SHAPE

Every girl is like a unique flower that unfolds its petals at a different speed and time, and the same is true for your body as it goes through its changes. Let's delve into one of these changes - the growth spurt. Now, you might be wondering what a growth spurt is. Well, in simple terms - it's a period of rapid growth in height and weight that takes place during puberty. During a growth spurt, it's pretty normal to feel that your clothes and shoes are getting way too tight, almost as if you outgrew them overnight. You might also feel a bit clumsier than usual, as if you're not quite used to your new body size or proportions yet - and that's totally okay. It's your body's way of adjusting to the changes. But what causes these growth spurts? These rapid changes in your body are driven by the signals sent from your brain to your glands to release hormones. Hormones are like special messengers in your body that tell different parts of your body what to do and when. The main ones at work here are your growth hormones, which give your body the 'go-ahead' to grow.

To give you a clearer perspective:

★ Usually, growth spurts in girls typically start between the ages of 8 and 13.

★ On average, girls grow between 5 to 20 centimeters (2 to 8 inches) in a year during their growth spurt.

★ Weight gain may also occur, as your body is preparing to tend to the developments of puberty.

Nutrition plays a crucial role in supporting these growth changes too! Protein, calcium, vitamin D, and healthy carbohydrates are particularly important. So do ensure to nourish your body well with plenty of fruits, vegetables, dairy, lean proteins, and whole grains. And like snowflakes, no two growth spurts are alike. Some girls might have their growth spurt in the early stages of puberty, while for others, it might come later. Your final height, however long it takes you to get there, is determined by your genes. In other words, it mostly depends on how tall your family members are. For some of you, the growth spurts might feel exciting. Your body starts to resemble more of the adults around you, less like a child's. But for others, it might feel somewhat awkward or uncomfortable. Both feelings are completely normal. Remember, it's your personal journey to adulthood, and everyone experiences it differently.

Remember, there are a few things that can help you manage your growth spurt better:

★ Get plenty of sleep. Your body uses this time to grow and repair itself.

★ Keep a balanced diet. As said earlier, your body needs many nutrients to grow, so don't skip meals!

★ Regular exercise helps support your bones and muscles as they grow.

It's essential to understand that different doesn't mean bad. Some girls may complete their growing sooner and some later, but each girl's timing is just as perfect as it is unique. Embrace these changes as they come; they are your steps towards blossoming into a young adult. Curiously and fearlessly, let's continue to unfold the mysteries and magic of growing up together. Everyone's body is unique and changes at its own pace and in its own way. This is the very core of body diversity. It's crucial to understand that there's a whole range of "normal" when it comes to health, fitness, and body shape, size, or type. So let's delve deeper into the science as to why your body is changing shape in a way that is special and unique to you.

As you hit puberty, your body starts producing hormones, namely estrogen in girls, and testosterone in boys. When it comes to estrogen, it's a key player in developing your reproductive system. But, it also plays a significant role in body changes, including the accumulation of body fat. So, when your body starts producing enough estrogen, it signals your body to increase fat storage for possible pregnancy in the future. This might cause your hips to become wider, and you may notice yourself becoming curvier. How your body fat is distributed also depends on your genetics. Just like you may have inherited your mom's eyes or your grandpa's laugh, you might also inherit body shape and size tendencies. There's a wide range of body types from the more rounded endomorph, to the lean and long ectomorph, and the muscly mesomorph. It's vital to remember that your body type doesn't define your health or your worth.

Nutrition plays a significant role in how your body changes too. Balance is key here. Many different nutrients, from protein to healthy fats, play a role in supporting growth and development during puberty. Finally, your level of physical activity can influence your body shape to a certain extent. Regular exercise can help you to build muscle and maintain a healthy body weight, as well as ensuring all your systems, including your heart and your bones, are strong and healthy. So, while each girl's body changes at a different speed and in different ways, it's important to assure you that you are perfectly normal. It is okay to love your body just as it is, because it's doing an amazing job growing and changing. There might be pressures from society, the media, or peers to look a certain way. However, it's important to keep in mind that your body and the changes it's going through are unique and normal for you. It's part of your body's preparation for becoming an adult. In a world full of different shapes, sizes, and colors, embracing body diversity and accepting the changes in your body is the key to maintaining a positive body image and a healthy mind.

Journal Exercise:

Draw a picture of yourself as you see yourself now. Next to it, write five words that describe the feelings you have about your body. Then, draw a picture of how you think you may look in three years time. Write five feelings or thoughts you think you might have about your future self. Reflect on how these feelings may change as you continue growing taller, gaining weight, or changing in shape. Remember, every body is unique and there isn't a 'perfect' body shape or size. Based on this chapter, what would you say to another girl who feels uncomfortable about changes in her body? Write a supportive message to encourage her.

☆ 2.6 HYGIENE AND TAKING CARE OF YOURSELF

Maintaining your personal hygiene is a crucial part of growing up. As your body starts to change during puberty, you may notice that you need to take extra care of your cleanliness and health. This doesn't need to be something difficult or confusing, let's break it down and make it as simple as ABC, starting with the A's.

'A' stands for Attention. Paying attention to your body is the first step in excellent hygiene. Look for any new changes, like sweat or body odor, and adjust your routine accordingly. For example, if you start noticing that you are sweating more, it might be a good idea to take more frequent showers or start using a deodorant

'B' stands for Body care. As your body changes, it's essential to keep your skin, hair, and nails clean. This means using suitable products for your skin type, washing your hair regularly, and keeping your nails short and clean.

'C' stands for Care. In addition to keeping your body clean, it's also important to take care of your overall health. This includes eating a healthy diet, getting enough sleep, drinking plenty of water, and staying physically active. This will give you the energy you need to grow and develop properly.

Remember, personal hygiene is a vital part of growing up and taking care of you. It's something to embrace and enjoy, not something to be worried or embarrassed about. As you guide yourself through these ABCs of hygiene, you will be well on your way to establishing a routine that makes you feel confident, comfortable, and healthy. Just like the rest of your body, your skin, hair, and nails are constantly evolving, and this is particularly pronounced during puberty. To help you navigate these changes, it's essential to learn about some strategies to care for these vital body parts.

Did you know that the largest organ of your body is actually your skin? With puberty comes many skin changes due to new hormonal productions, which can cause an increase in oils. This may lead to breakouts or acne. Don't worry, it's very normal, and there are ways you can help manage it:

★ Always try to keep your skin clean and hydrated. A daily regime can be as simple as washing your face twice daily with a gentle, fragrance-free soap, and then applying a moisturizer that's right for your type of skin.

★ Try not to pick or pop pimples. It can make them worse and also lead to long-term skin scarring.

Your hair too will undergo changes. You might notice it becoming oilier or, on the other hand, more dry. Here are some tips for hair care at your age:

★ Wash your hair every two to three days. Over-washing can lead to dryness, while under-washing can cause buildup of natural oils, dust, and sweat.

★ Use mild and gentle hair care products. Try to avoid those laden with harsh chemicals.

★ Healthy eating is key. Foods that are rich in vitamins like A, C, D, and E, and proteins can help nourish your hair from the inside.

Your nails, believe it or not, can also be affected during puberty. Growth rate increases, and sometimes new vertical or horizontal lines can appear on the nails. To keep your nails healthy and strong, follow these tips:

★ Don't bite your nails. It can expose your nails to infections.

★ Make sure to keep your nails clean and dry to prevent bacteria from growing under your nails.

★ Include a balanced diet with plenty of vitamins and minerals, especially vitamin B and iron.

Remember, it is okay to be more diligent with your new aging skin, hair, and nails during this phase. However, it is important to know that everybody's puberty journey is unique. There is no need to compare yourself with others. Each of your bodies is on its own schedule, so patience and self-care are crucial during this period. At the end of the day, make sure you are comfortable and confident with these changes because they signify your beautiful journey from a girl to a young lady.

Journal Exercise:

1. List three new things you learned about personal hygiene from this chapter. How can you incorporate these into your daily routine?

2. Write a paragraph about why you think it's important to maintain good hygiene especially during puberty.

3. Describe a situation where you faced a hygiene related challenge. Now, based upon what you've learnt from this chapter, how would you handle it?

4. Draw a simple chart showing your intended morning and evening hygiene routines incorporating the practices discussed in this chapter.

5. Write a letter to your future self explaining the importance of hygiene and the personal hygiene habits you hope to maintain as you grow older.

THE PERIOD TALK

☆ 3.1 WHAT IS MENSTRUATION?

One of the most significant changes that kick-start the journey to womanhood is the arrival of menstruation. However, it often seems a bit mysterious, doesn't it? In order to understand what's happening to your body, it's important to know the biology behind menstruation. Your body is a remarkable machine. It has an internal system that helps it grow, restore, and perform various functions. Like other body functions, menstruation is a part of this system. Your periods, also known as menstrual cycles, are an indication that your body is mature enough to potentially carry a baby.

It all begins with your brain sending signals to your body to release hormones, mainly estrogen and progesterone. These hormones are like messengers, telling your body to perform certain functions. Estrogen, in this case, is responsible for triggering the ovaries, which are tiny organs about the size and shape of an almond, residing on both sides of the uterus, to develop and release eggs. The release of an egg is called ovulation. One of the two ovaries produces and releases an egg each month. Once this egg is released, it's captured by the fallopian tube and makes a journey toward the uterus. This usually happens about two weeks before your period starts. While this is happening, the hormone progesterone continues its job of instructing your body. It specifically tells the uterus to prepare for the arrival of the fertilized egg. In response, the lining of your uterus - the endometrium - thickens with extra blood and tissue to create a comfortable and nourishing environment for a potential fetus.

Now let's talk about 'if' the egg gets fertilized. If a sperm manages to reach the egg during this journey and fertilizes it (which means it combines with the egg to create a single cell called a zygote), this cell will stick to the lining of your uterus and begin the process of growth into a baby. If this happens, that thick, cozy layer prepared by the uterus will be used to protect and nourish the developing baby. And that's basically how a pregnancy begins. However, if the egg does not get fertilized, it disintegrates. As a result, your body no longer needs the thick layer in the uterus. So, it sheds this layer. This shedding is what we know as menstruation or your period. It goes out from your uterus through the cervix and vagina and leaves your body as menstrual fluid. This process usually lasts between three to seven days. Then, the whole cycle begins again.

It's important to remember that every girl's experience with menstruation is different - what works for one may not work for another. There's no right or wrong way of embracing this significant change in your body. However, here are some practical tips that may help you: First, try to keep track of your period cycle. You can use a diary, a calendar, or even one of the many period-tracking apps available. This will help you predict when your next period may arrive, meaning you can be ready for it. Dressing comfortably during your period can help as well. Some girls find that loose clothing, such as sweatpants, can make them feel more comfortable and less restricted. You probably know that good personal hygiene is important, but it's especially vital during your period. Always make sure to change your pad, period underwear, or tampon every few hours (or more frequently, depending on your flow). Regular showers are also essential to keep you feeling fresh.

So, what about those emotions that you might experience? It's perfectly normal to feel a bit on edge or emotional during your period due to those pesky hormones. If you start to feel overwhelmed, take a few deep breaths, talk to someone you trust about what you're feeling or try writing your thoughts and feelings down in a journal. Getting some regular exercise may help too - it can boost your mood and help with any discomfort or cramps. Lastly, always keep an emergency kit in your school bag or locker. Include sanitary products, wet wipes, painkillers for cramps, and an extra pair of underwear. That way, even if your period surprises you, you'll be ready for it! Remember, this is a completely normal part of growing up. It might still feel new and daunting, but over time, things will get easier and more manageable. You're not alone, every girl goes through this, and there are always people around you who can and want to help. Don't hesitate to talk to your friends, mother, an older sister, or a teacher if you have any concerns.

Journal Exercise:

1. Write down three new things you learned about menstruation from this chapter.

2. How does knowing more about menstruation make you feel about going through puberty?

3. Write a letter to your future self about what you learned today. Include your thoughts, fears, and hopes about menstruation.

4. What are some of the questions, if any, you still have about menstruation, even after reading this chapter?

5. Can you think of three ways to talk about menstruation to a friend who might not have learned about it yet without feeling embarrassed or afraid? Write them down.

6. Imagine a world where no one feels uncomfortable speaking about menstruation. What kind of discussions would be happening? Jot down a few ideas.

7. Many cultures and societies have myths or superstitions about menstruation. Can you think about a positive and empowering menstruation myth? Or how would you change one of the negative myths you've heard into a positive one?

Be as creative and detailed as you want with your answers. Remember, there are no right or wrong responses!

☆ 3.2 PREPARING FOR YOUR FIRST PERIOD

You've already learned about the science of periods, but how can you prepare for this new, monthly adventure? Even though it may feel a little mysterious or even daunting, with some preparation and knowledge, you can handle it like a champ. Let's dive into the preparations!

Understanding the Signs

Before your first period arrives, your body might send you some signals. Some girls notice:

A clear or whitish discharge from the vagina. This is normal and can start months or even a year before your first period.

Tenderness or slight pain in the lower abdomen. Not every girl feels this, but some do.

Mood swings or heightened emotions. Remember, hormones can affect emotions. So if you're feeling a bit more moody or emotional, it could be a sign.

Gathering Your Supplies

It's always good to be prepared. Here's what you might want to have on hand:

Pads or Sanitary Napkins: These are absorbent materials you place in your underwear. There are many varieties - some are thicker for heavier days, and some are thin for lighter days or as panty liners for any day.

Tampons: They're used by some girls, especially during sports or swimming. If you're considering them, it's okay to talk to an adult or read more about proper usage.

A small pouch: This can be handy to store a pad or two, so you have it with you in your school bag or locker, just in case.

Knowing When It Might Start

There's no set age for everyone, but often, girls get their first period about 2 years after their breasts start to develop or after they notice that clear/whitish vaginal discharge.

Staying Calm

It's natural to feel a mix of emotions. You might be excited that you're growing up or nervous about this new change. Remember, every woman goes through this. It's a natural process and a sign that your body is working just as it should.

Having a Trusted Adult to Talk To

Whether it's your mom, older sister, aunt, teacher, or school nurse, it's great to have someone to ask questions or share your feelings with. They've been through it too and can offer advice, reassurance, or simply a listening ear. Your first period is a significant milestone in your journey to becoming a young woman. While it may seem a little overwhelming now, with preparation and understanding, you'll navigate this phase with confidence. Remember, this is a natural part of life, and you're never alone in it. Everyone is here to support you, and this book is a trusty guide to answer any questions you might have. So, embrace the change, and remember: You've got this!

Keeping a Period Journal

One super helpful tip that many girls find beneficial is keeping a period journal. Documenting the changes and patterns of your menstrual cycle will help you become more familiar with your body's unique rhythm.

Dates and Duration: Start by noting down the date your period begins and ends. Over time, you'll get a sense of its regularity.

Symptoms: Some girls experience symptoms like cramps, bloating, or headaches. By jotting them down, you can notice patterns and be better prepared for next time.

Emotions: Track any significant mood shifts. Understanding the emotional ebb and flow can be empowering.

Finding Comfort

Sometimes, periods can come with discomfort. Here are a few comforting tips:

Warmth: Using a warm heating pad or a hot water bottle can help soothe cramps.

Gentle Movement: While you might not feel like doing a lot, simple stretches or light yoga can alleviate some period symptoms.

Stay Hydrated: Drinking plenty of water can reduce bloating and keep you feeling good.

Selecting the Right Products for You

Over time, you'll find that certain sanitary products work better for you than others.

Eco-friendly Options: Apart from regular pads and tampons, there are reusable pads, menstrual cups, and period underwear. These can be both eco-friendly and cost-effective.

Trial and Error: Every body is different. It might take a few cycles to figure out which products you're most comfortable with.

Creating a 'Period Kit'

Apart from your usual supplies, consider adding:

Spare Underwear: Accidents happen, and that's okay. Having a spare can make you feel more secure.

Pain Relievers: Over-the-counter pain relievers can help with cramps, but always consult with an adult before taking any medication.

A snack: Some girls feel a dip in energy, so having a small, healthy snack can be a boost.

Learning about Nutrition and Periods

Believe it or not, certain foods can help alleviate period symptoms.

Iron-rich foods: Menstruation leads to a loss of iron. Foods like spinach, beans, and red meat can help replenish it.

Limit Caffeine: It can make some symptoms worse, like breast tenderness or anxiety.

Lastly, Sharing and Learning

Your friends are going through this too. Sharing experiences and tips can be both comforting and enlightening. This journey of understanding and embracing your period is not one you walk alone. It's a shared experience among women, connecting you in a unique way. Embrace the changes, learn continuously, and remember to be kind to yourself every step of the way.

UNDERSTANDING THE CHANGE	NECESSARY PREPARATIONS	MENTAL AND EMOTIONAL PREPARATION
Physical Changes in the Body	Stock up on Sanitary Products	Understanding and accepting the change
Menstrual Cycle Details	Discussing with a Trustee	Overcoming the fear and anxiety
Predicting the Start	Preparing a Period Kit	Developing a Positive Mindset
What to Expect During	Learning how to use Sanitary Products	Embracing the change

UNDERSTANDING THE CHANGE	NECESSARY PREPARATIONS	MENTAL AND EMOTIONAL PREPARATION
Handling Irregularities	Keeping an Open Line of Communication	Building a Support System

Journal Exercise:

Think about the information you've learned in this chapter about getting your first period. Take a moment to reflect on your feelings and thoughts.

1. How do you feel about experiencing your first period? Note any emotions you may be experiencing, be it excitement, anxiety, curiosity, or anything else.

2. What is one thing you found most enlightening in this chapter about preparing for your first period?

3. Write down one or two questions or concerns you still have about getting your first period.

4. List three ways you will prepare for your first period based on the advice in this chapter.

5. How will you help a friend or sibling who is going through the same experience? Write down any tips or advice you'd like to share.

Remember, every single girl experiences this and it's a natural part of becoming a woman. You are not alone. You're brave and strong just for reading and educating yourself about it!

☆ 3.3 MANAGING YOUR PERIOD

Now that you're familiar with the onset of your menstrual cycle, the next step is understanding how to manage it with ease.

While every girl's experience with her period is unique, certain strategies can make the monthly journey smoother for just about everyone.

Understanding Flow Variation:

Throughout your period, you may notice that some days you have a heavier flow, while on others it's lighter. This is normal. Being prepared with different absorbency products for these fluctuations will ensure you're comfortable.

Period Tracking Apps:

While a journal is a classic way to track your menstrual cycle, there are numerous apps available designed for period tracking. These apps often provide predictions about your next cycle, ovulation days, and more, making it easier to plan and prepare.

Maintaining Good Hygiene:

Change your sanitary product every 3-4 hours, or as needed depending on your flow, to maintain freshness and avoid potential health issues. Using mild, unscented soap can help in keeping the intimate area clean without causing irritations. Ensure you wash your hands before and after changing your sanitary product.

Disposal of Sanitary Products:

Dispose of sanitary products properly. Wrapping them in toilet paper or using disposal bags before placing them in the trash is recommended. Flushing tampons or pads can clog plumbing systems.

Comfort Measures:

Gentle exercises like walking or yoga can help alleviate cramps for some. Drink herbal teas, like chamomile, which can be soothing and help reduce menstrual pain. Ensure you get adequate rest. Your body is going through a lot, and a little extra sleep might be beneficial.

Dressing Comfortably:

Some girls prefer loose clothing during their period, especially if they experience bloating. Wear what makes you feel comfortable and confident.

Managing Leaks:

Wearing darker colored clothing can be a safety measure against visible stains. If you're worried about nighttime leaks, consider using a higher absorbency pad or tampon, or try period underwear designed for overnight protection.

Dietary Considerations:

Certain foods can help with period symptoms. For instance, consuming less salt can reduce bloating, while calcium-rich foods may help with cramps. Also, maintaining a balanced diet ensures you're replenishing nutrients lost during menstruation.

Seek Medical Advice if Needed:

While periods are a natural process, if you notice anything unusual about your period or if the pain becomes too much to handle, it's important to consult a medical professional. They can offer insights tailored specifically to your needs.

Support Systems:

Talking to friends, family, or trusted adults can provide additional tips, and it's reassuring to know that you're not alone in your experience.

Remember, managing your period is a learning experience, and it's okay to seek help or ask questions whenever you're unsure. With time, you'll find the routines and methods that work best for you.

PERIOD ESSENTIALS	EXPLANATION	SOLUTIONS
Menstrual Cycle	Your body's monthly cycle of preparing for a possible pregnancy	Track your cycle to predict periods
Sanitary Products	Items used to manage period blood	Experience with pads
Cramps	Pain felt in the lower abdomen due to your uterus contracting	Regular exercise and warm compresses can provide relief
Bloating and Emotional Changes	Hormonal fluctuations that affect your mood and body	Balanced diet and mindfulness to manage
Period Health Problems	Issues with periods that require medical attention	See a doctor if periods are too painful
Environment Friendly Options	Consciously choosing products that do not harm the environment	Consider reusable menstrual cups and period panties

Journal Exercise:

1. Write down five words that describe how you felt when you first learned about menstruation or periods.

2. Now, describe what, if anything, makes you feel nervous or uneasy about having a period.

3. What are some of the steps you can take to manage those concerns? Think about tips or strategies we discussed in this chapter.

4. How can you help a friend who might be nervous about getting her period? Write down three supportive things you could tell her.

5. Self-care during a period is important. List down two activities that you think could help you feel more comfortable during your period.

6. How can talking openly about periods and changes at puberty help us? Why is it important to discuss these topics?

Think carefully about your answers, giving yourself permission to express both positive and negative feelings. Remember, there's no right or wrong here – it's all about understanding and adapting to the changes that occur during puberty.

☆ 3.4 COMMON CONCERNS AND QUESTIONS

With the onset of menstruation comes a variety of questions and concerns. While every girl's experience is unique, certain questions seem to be almost universal among those who are navigating this new phase of life. Here are some of the most common ones, along with answers to provide clarity:

Is my period too heavy or light?

Menstrual flow can vary greatly among individuals. What might be heavy for one person could be considered normal for another. However, if you find yourself soaking through a pad or tampon every hour for several consecutive hours, it might be a good idea to consult with a healthcare professional.

Why is my menstrual blood a different color?

Menstrual blood can range from bright red to dark brown. The color can change depending on where you are in your cycle, with darker blood typically indicating older blood that took longer to exit the body.

Am I the only one feeling so emotional?

Hormonal fluctuations during your period can cause a roller coaster of emotions. It's perfectly normal to feel more sensitive or emotional around your menstruation time.

Why do I get cramps and how can I manage them?

Menstrual cramps are a common side effect of the uterus contracting to help shed its lining. While some discomfort is normal, intense pain should be discussed with a doctor. Over-the-counter pain relievers, heat packs, and certain dietary changes can help manage mild to moderate cramps.

Is it normal to have clots in my period blood?

It's not uncommon to see small clots or thicker bits of menstrual tissue during your period, especially on heavier days. However, if you're consistently noticing large clots, it might be worth discussing with a healthcare provider.

Why is my cycle irregular?

Many factors can influence the regularity of menstrual cycles, especially during the first few years of menstruation. Stress, diet, exercise, and certain medical conditions can all impact cycle regularity. If you're concerned, seek advice from a healthcare professional.

Can I do sports or swim during my period?

Absolutely! While some might feel less energetic during their period, physical activity can actually help alleviate cramps and improve mood. If you're swimming, consider using a tampon or menstrual cup for leakage prevention.

Do I need to see a doctor about my period?

Regular check-ups are always a good idea, but if you have specific concerns about your period - such as severe pain, very heavy flow, or missed periods without reason - it's essential to consult a medical professional.

When will my period become regular?

It can take several years after your first period for your menstrual cycle to settle into a regular pattern. Factors like stress, weight changes, and activity levels can also influence regularity.

Can I get pregnant during my period?

While it's less common, it is possible to become pregnant if you have unprotected intercourse during your period, especially if you have a shorter cycle or if your period lasts longer.

Remember, every person's body is different, and these answers might not cover every individual experience. Always listen to your body and seek advice from trusted adults or medical professionals if you have concerns or questions about your period.

CONCERN	EXPLANATION	TIPS
Cramps during menstruation	Pain in your lower abdomen or back is common during periods due to uterine contractions.	Use a heating pad to alleviate discomfort. Exercise can also help.
Heavier or lighter periods	Flow can vary person to person and even month to month.	Nothing to worry about.
Premenstrual Syndrome (PMS)	Happens days before your period, symptoms may include mood swings.	Try to reduce stress in your day to day life.
Periods haven't started yet	On average girls start their periods between 9 and 16 years of age.	Everyone's body is unique and develops on its own timeline.
Irregular periods	In the first few years after menstruation begins long cycles are common.	A period tracking app might help to better understand cycle length and irregularities.

Journal Exercise:

1. Jot down three things you learned from this chapter that surprised you or eased your worries about the ‚Period Talk'. What made these particular points stand out?

2. Write a mini letter to your future self, addressing common concerns about starting your period. Reassure your future self using the knowledge you've gained from this chapter.

3. Can you recall any situations where you or a friend had misleading or wrong information about periods? How would you handle these situations now, after reading this chapter?

4. Create a list of five questions you still have after reading this chapter. Try to research and answer at least two of these questions.

5. Imagine you are explaining what periods are to someone younger or a peer who does not know. Use the information from this chapter to write out a clear, simple explanation.

6. Reflecting upon the chapter, what aspects of having a period do you feel more confident about now? Are there any aspects you are still worried about? Why? Can you think of strategies to handle these worries?

Chapter 4

YOUR EMOTIONS AND MENTAL HEALTH

☆ 4.1 MOOD SWINGS AND EMOTIONAL CHANGES

Mood swings are a normal part of growing up, especially when you're going through puberty. They can seem mysterious or even scary at times, but don't worry, it's all part of the journey of becoming a young woman. Let's shed some light on what's going on in your brain during these emotional roller coaster rides. During puberty, your brain is going through rapid and major changes. This process is influenced by hormones, the body's chemical messengers, which are secreted in higher amounts during puberty. The brain is impacted by the increase in two hormones in particular: estrogen and progesterone. Estrogen can make you feel more emotional and sensitive, while progesterone can cause feelings of calm or even moodiness.

These hormones affect the part of your brain responsible for your mood and emotions, the limbic system. This system includes the amygdala, an almond-shaped structure that has a big role in managing your emotions and making sense of them. Now that you're going through puberty, your amygdala is processing lots of emotions, many of them for the very first time. So when you're experiencing mood swings, it's because your brain is adjusting to these new levels of hormones and trying to navigate all these brand new feelings. You might have times when you feel so joyful and excited, and other times when you feel quite low, upset, or even just a bit 'meh'. That's all okay and perfectly normal! Something as simple as not getting enough rest or having a lot of schoolwork can make these mood swings feel more intense. Lack of sleep makes it harder for your brain to handle stress and manage emotions, and academic pressure can easily lead to feelings of anxiety or overwhelm.

So, these are a few simple but key things to remember about mood swings:

★ They're caused by hormonal changes in your brain.

★ Lack of sleep and stress can make mood swings feel more intense.

Every girl going through puberty will notice that there are a lot of changes happening. Not all of these changes are physical ones that you can see. Some are emotional, and these changes can often be just as, or even more, confusing than the physical ones. You might find that one minute you're happy, and then all of a sudden, you're upset or angry without any clear reason, this is completely normal and a part of growing up. One important thing we need to remember is that puberty is a roller coaster of emotions because of your body's changing hormone levels. You're likely to feel things more intensely, and emotions can change quickly. This might include feeling:

★ Upset and crying over things that might not have bothered you before.

★ Moody and irritable.

★ More sensitive to what people say or do.

★ Mood swings, from feeling happy one moment to sad the next.

★ More self-conscious, particularly about your physical changes.

★ Stress and anxiety, particularly about dealing with all these changes.

Now, let's talk about some ways to handle these feelings. This may seem difficult, but don't worry, you're not alone in experiencing these emotions, and there are ways to manage them.

1. Practice mindfulness: This is about paying attention to the present moment without judgment. There are many ways to practice mindfulness, such as focused breathing, or spending quiet time in nature. By practicing mindfulness, you can help calm your thoughts and emotions.

2. Talk it out: It's important to express your feelings and not keep them bottled up inside. Talk to someone you trust, like a parent, a close relative, or a friend. Speak honestly about your feelings and what you're going through.

3. Write in a journal: Writing about your emotions can help you understand them better. You don't have to show this to anyone, it's for you.

4. Get creative: Channel your emotions into something positive, like painting, writing a story or playing an instrument. Plus, it's fun!

5. Physical activity: It's a natural mood-lifter. It could be anything from dancing around your room, joining a sports team or going for a bike ride.

6. Healthy eating and sleep: Good nutrition and enough sleep can have a positive effect on your mood. Aim for a varied diet and 8 to 10 hours of sleep every night.

Remember, your feelings are real and important. It's okay to feel a little up and down during puberty, and it's okay to ask for help if you are finding it tough to handle your emotions. Be patient and kind to yourself. These changes are part of your journey to becoming a young woman, and you are not alone. In time, these turbulent emotions will settle down, and you'll emerge stronger and more self-aware.

Journal Exercise:

Reflect on a day where you experienced mood swings. How did you feel, and what happened? What emotions did you go through? Now, apply what you've learned from this chapter. Can you think of a different way to handle your feelings if they occur again? Write about it. Also, list down five strategies you learned from this chapter that you think will help you manage your future mood swings better.

Furthermore, write a letter to your future self about how proud you are of her for navigating these emotional changes, what you hope she'll remember, and how you hope she'll continue to respond to her emotions.

Finally, think about your support system—who are the people you can turn to when you're feeling a lot of emotions? Write their names down and one quality in each of them that makes you feel safe and understood.

☆ 4.2 DEALING WITH STRESS

Stress - everyone experiences it, though it might feel like you're the only one struggling with it. Don't worry, you're definitely not alone. Stress is your body's way of responding to any kind of demand or threat. When you sense danger - whether it's real or imagined - your body's defenses kick in a rapid, automatic process known as the "fight-or-flight" reaction. This is your body's way of protecting you. When working properly, stress can help you stay focused, energetic, and alert. The science of stress is fascinating. Stress hormones, like adrenaline and cortisol, send energy to your muscles, heart, and other important parts of your body. This energy helps you to react quickly when you're in a dangerous situation. Nevertheless, while this fight or flight response helps to protect you in an emergency, a steady supply of these hormones without the need to react rapidly can cause problems. Stress isn't always a bad thing. It can help you meet daily challenges and motivates you to reach your goals. In fact, stress can help you accomplish tasks more efficiently. It can even boost memory. However, too much stress, or chronic stress, can lead to major health issues including anxiety, insomnia, muscle pain, high blood pressure and a weakened immune system. Imagine stress as the weight of a backpack. A little and your posture is better, making your stand tall. Too much and you can't stand up straight, it isn't healthy. That's how stress works. A moderate amount of stress can motivate you but too much stress can hold you down.

Worries about growing up and body changes are a common cause of stress for girls your age, but remember, everyone goes through these changes and it's perfectly normal to feel stressed at times. However, it's important to learn how to manage stress, as letting it build up can lead to problems with your overall health and emotional well-being. Remember, everybody experiences stress from time to time; it's a normal part of life. The key is to recognize when you're feeling stressed and find healthy ways to cope with it. You're stronger than you think! Keep this in mind as you continue to grow and change.

STRESSFUL SITUATION	COPING MECHANISM	OUTCOME
Homework overload	Break tasks into manageable chunks	Increased productivity
Fight with friend	Open discussion and apology	Restored friendship
Performance pressure in sports	Regular practice and positive affirmation	Improved skills
First period anxiety	Educate yourself	Reduced fear and increased preparedness
Poor grades	Extra study time	Improved understanding and grades
Moving to a new school	Join clubs to make new friends	Decreased loneliness and increased sense of belonging

Practicing meditation can create a sense of calm and focus that's so necessary during this stage of your life. There's no one right way to meditate; the most important part is setting aside a few minutes every day to sit quietly and focus on your breath. You can meditate in the morning when you wake up, at night before you go to sleep, or any time in between. It's your time to relax and just be.

Journaling is another effective way to manage stress. Writing down your feelings and thoughts can give you a fresh perspective, help you understand yourself better, and even boost your mood. You can write about anything you want - your day, your dreams, your worries, your goals. No one else is going to read it, so feel free to be completely honest.

Exercising regularly can also help manage stress. When you exercise, your brain releases chemicals called endorphins, which act as natural mood lifters. You don't have to do super intense workouts; any activity that gets your heart pumping will work. Try walking, dancing, biking, or yoga - whatever you enjoy!

Deep breathing is another effective stress relief technique. Whenever you're feeling anxious or stressed, take a few moments to take slow, deep breaths. Close your eyes, count to four as you breathe in through your nose, then count to four as you breathe out through your mouth. Repeat this a few times until you start to feel calmer.

Learning to manage your time can also help reduce stress. When you're feeling overwhelmed by too many tasks, it can help to make a schedule or a to-do list. Break down big projects into smaller, manageable steps, and stick to your plan as best as you can. It's okay if everything doesn't go perfectly; remember, it's about progress, not perfection.

Practicing mindfulness is another great way to unwind. Mindfulness is all about being fully present and engaged in the moment, rather than dwelling on the past or worrying about the future. This can be as simple as taking a few minutes to really savor your lunch, noticing the smell, taste, and texture, rather than wolfing it down while thinking about something else. Or taking a moment to appreciate the beauty around you, like the feeling of sun on your skin or the sound of birds chirping.

Also, don't underestimate **the power of a good night's sleep** for stress management. When you're well-rested, your mood is better, your mind is clearer, and you're better equipped to handle whatever comes your way. So, try to create a peaceful sleep environment and establish a regular sleep schedule that ensures you get enough rest. While you're navigating your way through these new experiences and changes, remember to take a step back, breathe, and give yourself the care you deserve. And always remember, it's okay to reach out for help if you're feeling especially stressed or overwhelmed. You're not alone, and there are many resources available to help you through this journey.

Journal Exercise:

1. Note down three situations or aspects in your life that currently cause you stress. They can be related to school, family, friends, or personal interests.

2. For each situation, write how it makes you feel, both physically and emotionally. Do you feel tired? Are you anxious or scared?

3. Share one technique or strategy you learned from this chapter that you think might help alleviate your stress in these situations.

4. Over the next week, try to implement these techniques when you face stress. After the week, write a follow-up entry reflecting on if and how these techniques worked for you. Has anything changed? How do you feel about these situations now?

5. Now imagine a friend is going through similar stress. Use what you've learned and your personal experience to advise her. What would you say to her?

6. Lastly, appreciate yourself for opening up about your stress and actively seeking solutions. Write three things

you love about yourself as a reminder of your strength and resilience.

☆ 4.3 BODY IMAGE AND SELF-ESTEEM

As you embark on this exciting journey of growing up, it's important to understand and embrace the physical changes that are about to take place. Some changes may be a little confusing, or even scary, but keep in mind, this is a normal part of growing up that every girl goes through. One of the first changes many girls notice is height. You might suddenly find yourself towering over your best friend or even some of your classmates. During the stage of puberty, you might grow significantly faster than you were used to, so don't worry if it seems like you need new clothes every other month. Your body shape will also begin to change. Expect your curves to develop more as your hips broaden and your waist narrows. Some girls also tend to put on a bit of weight during this phase, which is absolutely normal. So, remember not to stress over your changing figure and embrace your new body shape. Simultaneously, your breasts will start to grow. Also known as "budding," this is often the first sign of puberty. At first, you may notice small, tender lumps beneath your nipples. Gradually, over a few years, your breasts will continue to grow and fill out. Under your arms and around your genitals, you might even see some hair starting to sprout up. It can take up to a few years for all your hair to grow in, and when it does it may be thicker and darker compared to the hair on your head. In the middle of all these changes, you'll probably also start to sweat more. This is also perfectly normal - it's due to glands under your skin that begin to become active during puberty. But be sure to take extra care with your personal hygiene. Taking regular showers and using deodorant can keep you feeling fresh and confident. Sudden zits or acne might tag along with puberty too. The increase in hormone levels may cause your skin to become oilier and make you more prone to pimples. Good skincare regime and a balanced diet can help you keep these in check. This may seem like a lot to take in, and that's normal. You're not alone - every girl goes through this phase in some way or another. So take a deep breath, discover these changes, and embrace your journey into womanhood with open arms and an open heart.

Navigating the stormy seas of puberty is never easy, right? One moment you're giggling with friends over an inside joke and the next, you catch a glimpse of your reflection and wonder 'Who is that girl in the mirror?'. When you start seeing changes in your body and mind, it can sometimes be a bit scary or confusing. And hey, that's perfectly okay! Remember, it's a phase everyone goes through, and you're not alone. Let's talk about something incredibly important: self-confidence and self-esteem. They're like your secret superpowers. When these two are strong, you're able to face awkward situations and challenges with a smile. So, how do you boost these superpowers during times when everything is changing? Let's explore.

Step-by-Step Strategies for Boosting Self-Confidence and Self-Esteem:

★ Acknowledge Your Unique Strengths: Each of us is gifted in a unique way. Maybe you're good at drawing, or baking, or perhaps you're super good at solving puzzles. Identify your strengths and work on them - practice more, polish your skills, and always be proud of them. The recognition of your own abilities helps build confidence within you.

★ Positive Self-Talk: What do you say when you talk to yourself? Remember, your words matter. Encourage yourself with positive affirmations. Repeat to yourself, ,I am growing. I am capable. I am beautiful.' By doing so, you're programming your mind to believe in your own worth, and that will shine through as confidence.

★ Take Good Care of Your Body: A healthy body can lead to a healthier mind. Regular exercise, balanced meals, and good sleep habits can make you feel good about yourself. When you feel good on the inside, it reflects on the outside.

★ Foster Healthy Friendships: Surround yourself with positive people who value and respect you, for who you are. A good friend is someone who listens, encourages, and supports you without judgment.

★ Embrace Imperfections: Nobody's perfect, sweetheart, and that's what makes us humans. Your little quirks and personal shortcomings make you, you. Embrace them, celebrate them, and you'll love yourself more for it.

★ Create a Positive Environment: Decorate your personal space with things that you love, that make you happy. Fill it up with your favorite colors, pictures, books or even plants. It's your space, make it special!

★ Constant Learning: Embrace the mindset of learning. Each time you learn something new, you grow and that is amazing. Learn from your successes, your foes and most importantly, your own mistakes.

Harnessing the power of positive psychology and taking small steps to nourish your mind can go a long way in building self-confidence and self-esteem. Remember, like a butterfly coming out of a cocoon, this transition phase is necessary for your beautiful transformation. Embrace it with grace and courage, and don't forget to love yourself in the process.

Journal Exercise:

List three things you learned about body image and self-esteem from the chapter. How did these insights make you feel? Can you think of any ways you can apply these learnings in your daily life? Now list three things you love about your body, and three things you love about your personality. Remember, puberty is a journey, and everyone experiences it at their own pace. Note down one affirmation you can tell yourself whenever you start feeling unsure about your body changes.

☆ 4.4 FRIENDSHIP AND RELATIONSHIPS

Growing up is a journey full of many twists and turns, especially when it comes to navigating friendships. One day, getting along with friends feels so effortless. The next day, it might be confusing. Trust me, it's perfectly normal to experience such shifts in your social life, I promise to help you make sense of it all. Firstly, changes in friendships are common. As you are changing and growing up, so are your friends. Adolescence brings a new awareness and ways of thinking. You may develop different interests, hobbies, or even values from your friends. Sometimes, you and your friends might drift apart because of these changes. But that's alright! This time also opens opportunities for making new friends who share your newfound interests. Join clubs or participate in extracurricular activities, they are an excellent way to meet new people.

It's important to understand that friendships should be reciprocal. A good friendship is like a seesaw. Both sides give and take, pushing and pulling. There will be times when one person needs more support, that's OK. But overall, there should be a sense of balance. Remember, it's not your job to constantly take care of someone else's feelings, and vice versa. Misunderstandings or disagreements can happen. But real friends work it out by listening, apologizing when they're wrong, and forgiving one another. Honest communication is key to resolving these issues. If you find it's hard to communicate or if the friendship is leaving you drained or upset more often than not, then it might be time to reconsider the relationship. Along the ride of changing friendships, remember to always respect and value yourself. Don't change yourself just to fit in. True friends love and appreciate you for who you are. You deserve kindness, respect, and positivity so don't settle for less. Friendships can bring so much joy, laughter, and comfort. While there might be some hiccups along the way, remember that the journey is just as important as the destination. Cherish the good times, learn from the tough times, and know that every experience is helping you grow.

As you transition into puberty, you'll probably notice significant changes taking place in your emotional state as well. One day, you might feel on top of the world, and the next day, you might feel down in the dumps - for no apparent reason! Hormone changes can certainly have an impact on mood and feelings, causing you to experience a wide range of emotions. Some girls might feel more sensitive, weepy, or moody, while others may experience increased anxiety or irritability. Just know that it's perfectly okay to have these intense feelings. They are normal and a part of your growth. To gain control over your emotions, don't hesitate to try new strategies. Engaging in physical activity, practicing mindfulness exercises, or expressing your feelings through art, journaling, or talking with someone you trust can make a real difference.

Moving on to another significant aspect of growing up - relationships. You start to build a diverse network comprising not only friends but also teachers, mentors, and peers from extracurricular activities. It is essential to understand that every relationship should be rooted in respect and understanding:

   ☆ Respect: Every person deserves to be treated with kindness and politeness.

★ Understanding: It's important to be considerate about other people's feelings and perspectives. Often, you might have to agree to disagree - and that's perfectly normal!

When it comes to relationships, another crucial factor is setting healthy boundaries. A boundary is basically a rule or guideline that helps others understand what is acceptable behavior towards you. It's okay to say no when you're uncomfortable and to demand respect from everyone around you. Here are a few examples of healthy boundaries:

★ You don't have to hug someone if you don't feel like it.

★ You have the right to voice how you feel without fearing judgment.

★ You can opt to avoid engaging in conversations about personal topics you're not prepared to discuss.

Understanding that respecting these boundaries is just as important as setting them is an integral part of your journey towards emotional maturity. Let's explore the concept of healthy interaction. Healthy interaction with others can be fostered through effective communication. Be open and honest - if you're feeling upset or uncomfortable, it's okay to share these feelings instead of bottling them up. Additionally, it's valuable to practice active listening. This skill helps show that you care and respect the speaker's opinion. And most importantly, always aim for mutual respect in any interaction.

Journal Exercise:

Write about a recent experience where your feelings about a friendship or relationship changed. What happened to cause this change? How did it make you feel initially? How do you feel about it now?

Based on what you've just read in the chapter, discuss whether you handled the situation in a healthy way. If yes, write what you did right. If no, write what you could do differently in the future.

Write three things that you appreciate about your friendships or relationships. Can you identify any early signs of unhealthy relationships from the chapter? Are they present in any of your relationships?

Lastly, write down what you learned from this chapter, and how you intend to apply it to improve your relationships and mental health. Write it in the form of a commitment to yourself.

Chapter 6.3: Social Media and Self-Esteem

The digital age has revolutionized the way we communicate, share, and present ourselves to the world. Among the many platforms available, social media stands out as a dominant force shaping perceptions, interactions, and especially the way we view ourselves. For young girls navigating the delicate phase of puberty, understanding the relationship between social media and self-esteem is crucial. At its best, social media offers a platform for self-expression, connection, and inspiration. You can learn about different cultures, discover new interests, and even find role models. It's a space where communities form around shared interests and experiences. However, it also has a darker side. Constant exposure to perfectly curated images and lifestyles can lead to feelings of inadequacy, jealousy, or the belief that one's life isn't as exciting or fulfilling as others'.

One of the most significant pitfalls of social media is the constant urge to compare. With the endless stream of achievements, vacations, parties, and perfect selfies, it's easy to fall into the trap of feeling that everyone else has a better life.

Filtered Reality: Remember that what's posted online is often a highlight reel. Many of those 'perfect' moments are staged, filtered, and carefully selected from dozens of other, not-so-perfect shots.

Numbers Game: It's easy to get caught up in the numbers – likes, followers, comments. But your self-worth is not defined by these metrics.

Impact on Body Image:

During puberty, as your body undergoes numerous changes, social media can play a powerful role in shaping body image. Images of 'ideal' bodies can create unrealistic expectations and lead to dissatisfaction or even disorders like body dysmorphia. It's essential to:

★ **Diversify Your Feed**: Follow accounts that promote body positivity, represent diverse body types, and encourage self-love.

★ **Reality Check**: Understand that many images online are edited or altered. Even models don't look like their photos in real life!

★ **Boosting Self-Esteem in the Age of Social Media:**

★ **Digital Detox**: Taking regular breaks from social media can work wonders for your mental well-being. Even a short 24-hour break can help reset your perspective.

★ **Affirmations**: Create a list of positive affirmations about your qualities, achievements, and goals. Repeat these to yourself, especially when feeling overwhelmed by online negativity.

★ **Engage in Real-Life Activities**: Balance screen time with real-world activities that make you feel good, whether it's reading, sports, arts, or simply spending time with loved ones.

Setting Boundaries:

★ **Privacy First**: Adjust your privacy settings to control who can see your posts and personal information.

★ **Unfollow or Mute**: If an account consistently makes you feel bad about yourself or triggers negative emotions, it's okay to unfollow or mute them.

★ **Seek Support**: Talk to someone you trust if you ever feel overwhelmed by social media's impact on your self-esteem. Sometimes, just voicing your feelings can provide clarity.

Social media is a tool, and like all tools, its impact depends on how we use it. As you grow and evolve, your relationship with these platforms will change. Stay grounded in who you are, cherish real-world experiences, and remember that you are more than your online persona. In this age of digital connectivity, the most important connection remains the one with yourself.

NAVIGATING RELATIONSHIPS

☆ 5.1 FAMILY AND SIBLINGS

As we begin our journey through puberty, it's common to experience changes in how we relate to our parents, just as changes are happening in our bodies and minds. It can be a whirlwind of emotions, but with each new experience, we gain valuable understanding about ourselves and the world around us. Let's dive into some of these changes, the challenges they present, and how to navigate them. Throughout puberty, you might start to see your parents in a different light. This altered perspective can bring a bit of turbulence with it, but it's completely normal! It's a part of growing up - learning about individuality, independence, and forming our identities. You may have more debates or disagreements with your parents as your views become more diverse, or you might feel more sensitive to their comments or feedback. It's important to remember, these new dynamic isn't necessarily bad. It's just different. It's about shifting from a child-parent relationship to a more adult-like connection. It's natural to want a capacity to make your own decisions, and have them respected. In order to do so, communication is key. Talking about your feelings will not only help them understand you better, but it can also strengthen your relationship in the long run. Likewise, try to understand their perspective. This can lead to really fruitful discussions and it's a great opportunity for mutual growth.

Handy tips to mitigate these changes and challenges:

★ Establish open lines of communication: Be honest about the changes you're experiencing and how you feel about them. Admit when something they say or do affects you - it might be unintentional on their part.

★ Be patient: Your parents might need some time adjusting to your changing personality, just as you need time getting used to your changing body and emotions.

★ Search for mutual interests: Spending quality time together can strengthen your bond. It could be activities you both enjoy or exploring new hobbies together.

★ Find a balance: While you're asserting your independence, remember that your parents generally have your best interest at heart. Listening to their advice doesn't mean you're any less independent.

★ Seek professional help if needed: If the dynamics between you and your parents become very complicated or troubling, don't hesitate to ask for help. Schools often have counselors, or your doctor may also have resources.

Remember, these trials are part of the growing process not just for you, but for your parents too. Above all else, remember that love and understanding are fundamental keys to navigate these changes. You're not alone in this journey, so don't forget to reach out for help when you need it.

During your journey of growing up and the changes it brings, one thing you might not often think about is the impact it has on your relationship with your siblings. Your brothers and sisters can also be going through similar changes both physically and emotionally or they may be trying to understand your changing behavior. Here are some ways to manage this shift in your relationships. First and foremost, realize that everyone in your family is adapting to your growing independence and emotional changes. Everyone including your siblings need time to adjust. They might sometimes find your mood swings confusing or your need for more privacy strange. Remember, it's a time of change for them too, especially if they're younger. Try focusing on empathy. It can be hard when you're both going through changes, but everything is easier to deal with when you try and understand how the other person is feeling. Put yourself in your sibling's shoes. If they're older, they may feel protective and worried about you. If they're younger, they might feel left out or confused.

If arguments or disagreements arise, and they probably will, try your best to address them calmly. The changes you're going through might make it seem like every disagreement is a big deal. But remember, sometimes it's just not. Ask yourself whether the problem will matter in a year, a week, or even a day. If it won't, it's probably not worth a whole lot of stress. It's easy to lose sight of the bond you and your siblings share when things get difficult, but try to keep in mind all the things that make your relationship special. Maybe it's a shared love for a certain TV show, or identical laughs, or how you both can't stand broccoli, or a silly dance you made up together. If the changing dynamics become overwhelming, retreat to these shared experiences for comfort. Moreover, don't hesitate to communicate with them. If you feel comfortable, let your sibling know that you're going through a lot of changes and you might behave a little differently, but it doesn't change how much you care for them. Honest conversations can strengthen your relationship and increase understanding.

Your siblings can be your strongest supporters and your lifelong friends if you nurture these relationships effectively. Your journey through growing up might be a little bumpy, but with your siblings by your side, you're never alone in facing these changes. Feel reassured because every phase passes giving place to new bonds and shared experiences. Growing up is a shared journey and while it brings changes, it also brings new horizons of shared understanding and deeper connections. Above all, be patient with yourself and your siblings. You're all figuring things out and no one gets it perfect on the first try. Give yourself, and them, the grace to grow up at your own pace, in your own way. Life's a learning curve and your sibling relationships are part of that journey. Navigate it together, learn from each other, and as you all grow, allow your bonds to grow stronger too.

Journal Exercise:

1. Draw a family tree and include the names of your immediate family members and your relation to them.

2. Write down five things that you like about each of your family members, and also what you sometimes find challenging about them.

3. Reflect on the changes you are going through and how they might be affecting your relationships with your family. Are there any specific instances you can think of where this has occurred?

4. How do your siblings or parents help you deal with the changes and challenges of growing up? If you are an only child, who do you turn to?

5. Mention three ways you can help your family to better understand what you are experiencing during puberty.

There are no wrong answers. It is completely normal to have mixed feelings about family and siblings. The goals are to appreciate your family dynamics and understand the importance of love and support as you navigate puberty.

☆ 5.2 FRIENDS AND MAKING NEW ONES

Have you ever noticed how your friendship circle has evolved in recent times? That's because as we grow up, our friendships tend to morph and mature along with us, and puberty plays a significant role in this transformation. Friendship isn't just about having fun together anymore; it goes deeper, provided with a base layer of mutual understanding, shared experiences, emotional support, and trust. You may find that certain friends are becoming closer, while others may seem to drift away, and that's perfectly fine. As you enter this new phase, there can also be fluctuations in your friendships due to increasing sensitivity and heightened emotions.

What some may not realize is, puberty doesn't just alter your physical appearance, but it also impacts your emotions, thoughts, and thus, your social relations. Those whispering hormones molding your body are simultaneously shaping your emotions, making your feelings more intense and complex. During this time, you might feel a stronger need for privacy or experience more arguments with your friends. This is simply because everyone around you is going through the same phase, and everyone's learning to navigate this shifting landscape along with balancing their own changing emotions. Negotiating friendships in the time of puberty can be a challenge, but with understanding and patience, it's a challenge you can tackle. Remember, it's okay to take your time, ask for help, and communicate openly about your feelings.

In navigating any changes in your friendships, remember - you are not alone. Everyone around your age is learning too. Making new friends often feels like a daunting task, but it doesn't have to be. What's important is being kind, approachable, sincere, and being you. Here are a few methods and ideas to guide you on your journey to making new friends. Get involved, either in school or in your community. Join a club or team, volunteer in a campaign, help out in a community service. This not only gives you exposure to meet other kids your age but also introduces you to others who share similar interests. It's nice to know someone who you already have something in common with!

Confidence is key. Be brave and don't be afraid to approach someone first. A simple hello, a smile, or a wave is often enough to break the ice and spark a conversation. Remember, everyone appreciates friendliness and kindness, so being approachable and warm can go a long way.

Learn to actively listen. When you listen intently to what the other person is saying, not only does it mean that you value their thoughts, but it opens the conversation up to a deeper, more meaningful level. Being a good listener helps you become a good friend.

Celebrate individuality. Remember that everyone is unique, with their own qualities, strengths, and quirks. Embrace the differences in others - they make us more interesting! Plus, your new friend will likely appreciate you even more for it.

Be patient. Building relationships take time and effort, and don't let initial setbacks discourage you. The best friendships are those weaved over time, filled with shared experiences and trust.

Understanding and kindness go hand in hand. Not everyone you meet will have the same outlook or perspective as you, and that's okay! Practice empathy, put yourself in their shoes, and respect their feelings.

Bear this in mind, true friendships are never about how many friends you have. It's about the connections you make that are strong and meaningful, and the memories you create together.

Journal Exercise:

1. Write about a time you made a new friend. What was most exciting or scary about this process?

2. Reflect on a time when you had a disagreement with a friend. How did you both resolve it? What could you have done differently?

3. Are there qualities you think are very important in a friend? List them and talk about why they matter to you.

4. Do you ever feel nervous or unsure about how to start a conversation with someone new? Write about this experience and what you think can help you feel more comfortable.

5. Think about a friend you admire. What qualities do they have that you would like to develop in yourself?

It's perfectly normal and okay to have doubts or questions about new friendships. Always embrace kindness and empathy and don't forget that it's OK to learn as you go!

☆ 5.3 BULLIES AND PEER PRESSURE

There's no doubt that undergoing changes during puberty can sometimes be a challenging journey; it can be more difficult if you encounter something called "bullying." Bullying is a type of aggressive behavior where someone intentionally and repeatedly causes another person injury or discomfort. Now, this isn't some sort of battle game, but it's definitely something that needs to be tackled bravely. Let's take a look at ways to understand and overcome bullying. Consider for a moment that you're a detective. You're on a case to learn more about this 'bullying mystery.' The first important clue to understand is that bullying can comprise of various forms such as verbal (like calling names), physical (like hitting), and even cyber-bullying (like mean messages online). Another clue is that bullying usually involves a pattern or repeated behavior and includes an imbalance of power.

Getting a grasp of 'why' people bully can also form a big part of your detective puzzle. It can occur due to the bully dealing with their problems or insecurities, power-play, or even because they have been victims of bullying themselves. However, it's crucial for you to remember that no reason makes their actions right or fair. Now the part comes where you transform into a superhero standing your ground against bullies. Here are some strategies that might come in handy:

1. Become a Confidence Queen: Confidence can help you stand strong against bullies. Remember how awesome you are by thinking about all your amazing qualities. This will boost your shield of self-esteem.

2. Stand Tall, Speak Firmly: Your body language says a lot about you. Stand tall, maintain eye contact, and speak calmly and clearly to show that you're not an easy target.

3. Practice the ‚Buddy System‘: There's power in numbers. Sticking close to friends can discourage bullies.

4. Setting up Safety Zones: Spend time in areas where bullying is less likely to occur, such as near adults or in populated parts of school during breaks.

5. Use the ‚Stop, Walk, and Talk‘ method: First, say „Stop“ in a clear, powerful voice. Then, walk away from the situation to show it doesn't affect you. Finally, talk to a trustworthy adult about it.

6. Record and Report: It's important to keep evidence of bullying (like screenshots of messages) and share it with adults you trust, like parents and teachers.

7. Make sure to take care of yourself: It's important to heal by doing activities you love. Surround yourself with positive influences and consider talking to a professional if feelings of sadness or anxiety persist.

Everyone deserves respect, kindness, and the freedom to be ourselves. Also, know that it's okay to seek help. Bullying isn't just about the one being bullied and the bully; it's about all of us, our school, our community, and even our world taking a stand against it. It's about you and your wonderful, magnificent journey of growing up and becoming the incredible person you're destined to be. Remember the famous saying, "What doesn't kill you makes you stronger."

Developing resilience to peer pressure is something that everyone must learn, especially as we grow older. It can be a challenge when friends want you to do something you're not comfortable with or that you know is wrong. Here, let's explore some ways to cultivate a strong mindset and make positive choices when faced with peer pressure. Always trust your gut feelings. Sometimes, our bodies can tell us what our minds haven't quite registered yet. If your stomach is in knots or you're feeling anxious about something your friends are doing, it's usually a sign that it's not right for you. Listen to that inner voice and stand up for what you think is right. Forming a solid support network is essential. A support network can include your family, friends, teachers, or anyone else who has your best interests at heart. These individuals can provide excellent guidance and back you up when you must face challenging situations. They could also help you bolster your courage to make positive choices. Expressing your thoughts and feelings to others in a respectful manner is crucial. Talk about your concerns with someone you trust. Remember, it's okay to disagree with your friends, as long as you do it respectfully. Everyone makes mistakes. When you find yourself in a situation where you've given in to peer pressure and done something you're not proud of, remember that it's only human to make mistakes. What's more important is what you learn from these situations and how you grow. Use it as a learning experience to handle such situations better in the future.

Practice saying 'No.' Sometimes the most straightforward response is the best. If you are uncomfortable with a situation, voice your concerns and say 'no'. If they are truly your friends, they will respect your decision and not hold it against you. Develop your own set of values and principles. Having your own set of values can guide you towards what is right or wrong. This moral compass can help steer you in the right direction when faced with difficult choices. Being true to you is the most important of all. Don't change your behaviors or attitudes just to fit in. If it's unlike you, don't do it. You are unique, and your friends should appreciate you for who you are. Developing resilience to peer pressure is a journey, not a destination. It's okay if you make mistakes along the way. What's important is you learn from them, and each step, no matter how small, is progress. Remember, growing up is a magical journey, and it's okay to take your time. After all, everybody grows at their own pace.

Journal Exercise:

1. Describe an instance (if any) when you encountered bullying or peer pressure.

2. How did that experience make you feel? What emotions did you go through and how did you handle those feelings?

3. Identify three strategies from the chapter you could use if you encounter bullying or peer pressure in the future.

4. Choose one person in your life you feel comfortable discussing these topics with. Why do you trust this person?

5. Imagine your friend is facing bullies or peer pressure. Write a supportive letter for them applying what you

learned today. Remember to advice they seek help from trustworthy adults.

6. Finally, fill in the following: One thing I learned today about bullies and peer pressure that I wish all girls my age would know is _____.

☆ 5.4 CRUSHES AND ROMANTIC FEELINGS

Crushes are a kind of sweet mystery that often pop up during puberty. It's when you start finding a certain person particularly attractive or interesting. And the crazy part? They might not even know you exist! It's perfectly normal, though, and part of the rollercoaster ride of growing up. We call these feelings 'crushes' because, sometimes, they can feel a bit weighty, or as if they're 'crushing' you with loads of emotions - excitement, nervousness, happiness, and even a bit of confusion or fear. Crushes aren't always easy to handle, but understanding them can help. One typical sign of a crush is the sudden rush of 'butterflies in your stomach' when you see or think about this person. You see, when you have a crush, your body might respond in some strange ways. Your heart might beat faster, your palms may get sweaty, and you might even feel a swirling sensation in your stomach. Behind the scenes, your body is releasing chemicals and hormones, like adrenaline, which can trigger these reactions. It's your body's way of responding to strong emotions or excitement. It's the same reason your stomach might twirl when you're on an exciting theme-park ride or about to open a birthday present.

Crushes can be intense, but they're also temporary. They come and go. You might have a crush on one person one month, and then find someone else interesting the next month. That's completely okay and a normal part of growing up. It's okay to feel a bit overwhelmed by your crushes, especially at first. Even adults still get confused by their feelings sometimes.

Let's get this straight: Having a crush doesn't mean you're in love. Crushes can develop quickly and fade away even faster, while love is a deep emotional attachment that grows over time. It's okay to have crushes, but remember: They're not everything. Your feelings might feel strong and significant now, but they will change and evolve as you grow up. It's also important not to confuse a crush with true friendship. You can certainly have a crush on a friend, but it doesn't necessarily mean that it is love or that you should act upon these feelings. Sometimes it's best to just enjoy the friendship for what it is.

Stay true to yourself and remember: having a crush is just a part of life's grand adventure. As you grow and mature, there's a great chance that you might experience your first romantic feelings. It's normal, it happens to everyone, and it's a part of growing up. These new feelings may be exciting, confusing, or even a bit scary — but don't worry, you're not alone. Here are some tips to guide you in handling these new emotions:

Romantic feelings towards someone are natural as you mature. Even though it might feel strange or different, know that it's a perfectly normal part of growing up and there's nothing to be scared or ashamed of. It's essential to determine the difference between infatuation and love. When you have romantic feelings for the first time, it can be intense. Often, these feelings are infatuation — a strong but not lasting attraction. Love, on the other hand, is a deeper feeling that grows over time. Both feelings are okay to experience. Communicating your feelings is essential too. If you're ready and comfortable, telling someone about your feelings can help. This doesn't have to be the person you're attracted to. It could be your trusted adult, a close friend, a sibling. They can offer support, advice, or just a listening ear.

Always respect the feelings and boundaries of others. If you're developing feelings for a friend, remember that they might not feel the same way about you. If that's the case, it's okay. Respecting their feelings and boundaries is critical. Everyone develops at their own pace. Don't rush into things because you think that's what you should be doing. There's no set plan or timeline that you need to follow. Instead, focus on understanding how you feel and what you want. Prioritize yourself and your mental health. It's easy to get carried away with your feelings. Remember to also make time for hobbies, friends, family, school, and any other things you might love to do. Lastly, know that it's okay to be single. You don't need to be in a relationship to feel fulfilled or happy. Enjoy your own pace and don't let societal expectations influence your feelings. As you navigate this new stage of life, keep in mind that it's okay to feel uncertain or confused. It's a new experience, and it will take some time to understand these new feelings fully. Just remember, you're never alone in this journey, and it's perfectly okay to seek help or advice when you need it.

Journal Exercise:

Reflect on any new, different or stronger feelings you have been experiencing recently towards others around your age. Is there anyone who makes you feel super excited whenever you see or talk to them? Write a paragraph about these unique feelings and what you believe might be the reason behind them. Remember, having crushes is completely natural and it's absolutely okay to discuss them, especially here in your journal where it's only you and your thoughts.

Now, write down three questions about crushes or romantic feelings that you're still unsure about, don't know the answer to, or are curious to learn more about. We will revisit these questions later as you journey further into understanding your changing feelings and emotions.

Then, list down 2-3 things you learned from this chapter about crushes and romantic feelings. How do they help you understand your own feelings? Don't forget to be clear and honest with what you're experiencing. There's no right or wrong answer here, just your personal experience and thoughts.

☆ 5.5 ONLINE FRIENDSHIPS VS. REAL-LIFE FRIENDSHIPS

In today's digital age, many of your friendships might begin or flourish online. Sites like Instagram, TikTok, Snapchat, and even online gaming platforms can serve as places to connect with others, share experiences, and form bonds. It's wonderful that we have these tools, especially for those times when we're unable to meet in person. However, as with all things, it's essential to understand the nuances between online and real-life friendships.

Virtual Connections:

Online friendships often form around shared interests, hobbies, or activities. Perhaps you've joined a fandom community, connected over a multiplayer game, or bonded over a shared talent or hobby. These online spaces can be comforting and allow you to connect with like-minded individuals who you might not meet in your daily life. Remember, online friendships, like any other, require mutual respect, understanding, and trust. Just as in real life, you should feel comfortable and safe when chatting with online friends. Trust your instincts. If a conversation feels off or a person pushes for too much information, always prioritize your safety.

Depth vs. Breadth:

While you can have many online acquaintances, the depth of online friendships might be different from those you've developed face-to-face. Physical presence allows for shared experiences that can deepen trust and understanding. That's not to say that online relationships lack depth, but they might evolve differently.

Communication Dynamics:

The way we communicate online can differ from our face-to-face interactions. Without physical cues, like body language or tone of voice, misunderstandings can arise. Emojis and gifs are fun, but they can't replace the nuances of face-to-face chats. Make an effort to be clear in your online communications, and if you sense a misunderstanding, try to clear it up calmly.

Staying Safe:

With the internet's anonymity, it's paramount to prioritize safety. Remember the basics:

★ Avoid sharing personal details like your home address, school name, or other identifying information.

★ Use privacy settings to control who can view your profiles.

★ Never agree to meet an online friend in person without discussing it with a trusted adult.

Real-life Friendships:

While the digital world offers a realm of possibilities, nothing can quite replace the warmth of an in-person chat, the joy of a shared experience, or the comfort of a hug. Real-life friendships provide immediate emotional feedback, a deeper understanding of each other, and a shared history that strengthens bonds. That said, as you grow and change during puberty, so might your friendships. It's natural. Some friendships will evolve, while others might fade. Prioritize friendships that make you feel positive, supported, and valued.

Striking a Balance:

As you navigate the world of friendships during puberty, try to strike a balance between online and real-life connections. Both types of friendships offer unique experiences and opportunities for growth. Embrace the best of both worlds, always prioritizing safety and genuine connections. Remember, friendships, whether online or offline, should uplift and support you. Surround yourself with positive influences, and don't be afraid to reach out for help if you ever feel overwhelmed or uncertain about any relationship.

Chapter 6

HEALTHY HABITS FOR A HEALTHY YOU

☆ 6.1 NUTRITION AND EXERCISE

When you think of food, what comes to mind? Is it the sweet decadence of a chocolate chip cookie? The tart, succulent taste of a juicy orange? Food, in all its forms, is one of life's simplest yet profound pleasures. But it's not just about titillating your taste buds. The food you eat and the nutrients it provides play a significant role in your growth and development during puberty. Did you know that body changes like growing taller, the development of secondary sexual characteristics like breasts, wider hips for girls are all partially fueled by the foods you eat? How fascinating indeed! Let's break it down a bit. Your motor to keep running, to keep living, is energy. This energy is derived from the food you consume. When talking about energy, we cannot miss the principal sources – carbohydrates, proteins, and fats.

Carbohydrates are the body's main source of energy. They are found aplenty in foods like bread, cereal, and pasta. Energizing your body with these foods will help you succeed in school, sports, and other activities.

Proteins, on the other hand, act as the building blocks of life and are essential for growth. They support the building of cells, muscles, skin, nails, and hair. Consuming protein-rich foods such as dairy products, meat, fish, beans, or legumes can support all the physical changes you experience during puberty.

Fats often get a bad reputation, but they too are critical. Unsaturated fats like those found in avocados, nuts, and fish are heart-healthy and help your growing body absorb vitamins.

We also have **vitamins and minerals**, micronutrients that sustain many bodily functions. Vitamins like A, B, C, D, E, and K each have a unique role. They help maintain healthy skin, hair, and nails, boost immunity, and assist in the production of hormones, including those at play during puberty. Minerals like calcium, iron, and zinc are crucial as well. They strengthen bones (important for those sudden growth spurts!) and transport oxygen in the blood.

Fiber, another important component found in fruits, vegetables, and whole grains is essential for a healthy digestive system.

Now, it's easy to misunderstand this information and overload on a single food group. But the key to responsible nutrition is variety and balance. While it's crucial to intake all the nutrients we discussed, moderation is also vital. Excessive consumption of anything is not beneficial. Try to create a plate with different food groups to make sure you get a mix of these nutrients. Nutrition has a profound impact on your growing body during this transition. It fuels growth spurts, supports healthy skin, contributes to mood and cognitive functioning. With proper nutrition, your journey through puberty can be a smoother, more comfortable ride.

Exercise is the second important bit. Exercise isn't just a way to burn off energy or lose weight. It's like your secret weapon during puberty, helping you navigate the changes happening throughout your body. Engaging in regular physical exercise can support your body in various wonderful ways.

Exercise can help promote better sleep. Puberty can sometimes cause changes in your sleep pattern, and you might find it challenging to get a peaceful night's sleep. Regular physical activity has been shown to improve the quality of sleep and help you awake refreshed and recharged. Next, exercise can serve as a means to stabilize your emotions. As we go through changes, our emotions can sometimes feel as though they're on a roller coaster ride. Regular movement can release chemicals in your body called endorphins, which create feelings of happiness and euphoria. It's like a tiny dose of joy every time you break a sweat! Exercise can also help to build and strengthen your bones. Our bones grow rapidly during puberty, and weight-bearing activities like running, jumping, or strength training can increase your bone density. This will not only make you stronger now but also help to prevent osteoporosis in the future.

Speaking of strength, exercise during puberty can increase muscle development too. Your muscles are growing and changing just like the rest of your body. Engaging in activities that challenge your muscles can help to sculpt and strengthen them. This process can boost your confidence and self-esteem too! Moreover, physical activities can improve the health of your skin. As hormonal changes can make your skin oilier and prone to breakouts, engaging in exercise can help to control these conditions. Exercise increases blood circulation that can clear up your skin and give you a healthy complexion. Remember that healthy habits start young. By adopting fitness as a regular part of your routine now, you're setting yourself up for a lifestyle of good health and well-being down the line. So when you're feeling unsure or even a bit overwhelmed about all the changes happening in your body, remember that you have a secret weapon. Choose an exercise you enjoy. It could be anything from swimming, soccer, cycling, or dancing. Make sure to take good care of your body along the way, eating a balanced diet and drinking plenty of water. Your body is becoming the future you, and it deserves the best care and respect.

Journal Exercise:

1. Write down five foods that you learned are important for your growth and development. How do you feel about these foods and how will you include them in your diet?

2. Present one healthy nutritious dish you'd like to prepare and eat. Give a short explanation why you chose this meal.

3. Note down three benefits of exercise on your body during puberty as covered in the chapter. How will these benefits encourage you to stay active?

4. Reflect on your current physical activities. Are there any new forms of exercise you'd like to try? Discuss why.

5. Journal about any fears or worries you have regarding nutrition and exercise during puberty. What steps can you take to address these concerns based on what you learned in this chapter?

Remember, nothing changes overnight! It's about taking small steps towards a healthier, happier you.

☆ 6.2 SLEEP MATTERS

It's not unusual to feel impossibly sleepy as you start growing up. You might even find yourself sleeping in more on weekends, and that's because sleep plays an essential part in your transition into your teenage years. So curl up, get cozy, and let's dive into the fascinating science behind sleep and its major role in puberty. Your body goes to work while you're sleeping, especially during puberty. All those extra hours you find yourself needing are actually because your body is busy growing and changing while you sleep. One important thing occurring while you sleep is the release of a hormone known as the growth hormone. This is the very substance that aids in your physical growth during puberty, including the development of breasts, the widening of hips, and the growth of body hair.

As well as promoting physical changes, sleep also contributes to your brain's development. It aids in the creation of new pathways in your brain, helping you learn, remember information, solve problems, and cope better with change. Sleep deficiency, meanwhile, has links with mood swings and feeling low. You might find yourself more prone to pimples and feel sluggish in school if you aren't getting enough sleep. As you enter puberty, there might be changes in your sleep patterns. You may start staying up late at night and find it difficult to wake up early. It's like your body clock gets shifted, making you prefer later bedtime and wake times.

But the question remains, why do these changes happen? The precise reason isn't entirely clear, but it has to do with a hormone called melatonin. Melatonin is primarily responsible for regulating your sleep-wake cycle. As you approach your teenage years, the body starts making this sleep hormone later in the evening. This is why you may not feel tired even if it's late. In light of these changes, it's important to make sleep a priority, to ensure your body will function at its best. Here's how:

★ Have a consistent bedtime, even on weekends. Doing this can help to regulate your body's clock and could help you fall asleep and wake up more easily.

★ Wind down before bedtime. Try to set aside a period for relaxation before sleeping. Turn off electronic devices and engage in calming activities like reading a book or having a bath.

★ Make your room conducive for sleep: that means dark, cool, and quiet. Consider using earplugs, eye shades, or a fan to create an environment that suits your needs.

★ Limit naps to 20 minutes in the afternoon. While napping does not make up for inadequate nighttime sleep, a short nap of 20-30 minutes can help you feel more rested and alert.

Remember, lots of magic happens when you sleep, especially during puberty. Having a good understanding of the role of sleep during these transformative years and taking steps to ensure sound rest can help make your transition into teen-hood smoother. Having a good night's sleep is crucial during your phase of growth. It helps your body recharge, boosts your brain function, and keeps up your mood. Also, transformations inside your body are better carried out when you're asleep. Here are some simple methods you could adapt to establish healthy sleep habits:

★ Try to maintain consistency in your sleep schedule. Going to sleep and waking up at the same time every day can train your body to follow a regular rhythm. This results in better sleep quality over time. It's true that it can be challenging, especially on weekends and during holidays, but trust me, the benefits are well worth it.

★ Create a comforting and sleep-conducive environment for yourself. An ideal sleeping environment would be quiet, dark, and slightly cool. You could also add some personal touches like a favorite blanket or pillow. All these could help you transition smoothly into slumber.

★ Next, we must discuss electronics, as they are a major factor in sleep disturbance. Bright screens stimulate our brains and make it harder to fall asleep. So make it a rule to switch off all electronic devices at least an hour before bedtime. This could include a phone, computer, tablet, or television. Yes, this means no more late-night chats or binge-watching your favorite shows!

★ Pay attention to what you consume near bedtime. Avoid food and drinks that contain caffeine, such as soda, tea, chocolate, and certainly coffee. It's best to have your dinner at least a couple of hours before you sleep and try not to go to bed either too hungry or too full.

★ Exercise is also beneficial for your sleep, as it helps to tire you out and makes you more ready for bed. However, vigorous exercise close to bedtime can have the opposite effect by stimulating your body. So, find a balance and time your workout sessions wisely.

★ Establish a wind-down routine before bedtime. This might include activities that relax you, such as reading a book, drawing, listening to soft music, or even practicing some gentle yoga. This routine signals your body that it's time to start slowing down and get ready for sleep.

The take-home message is: Sleep is not merely a 'thing' you do but an essential part of you taking care of your growing body. So make it a priority.

Journal Exercise:

I. Write a short paragraph about the changes you have noticed in your sleep pattern lately. How does it compare to your sleep schedule prior to the start of puberty?

2. How does the quality of your sleep impact your day? Discuss both good and bad sleep days.

3. In the chapter 'Sleep Matters', several tips for getting better sleep are shared. Which ones do you think you can start implementing and why?

4. Reflect on how much technology impacts your sleep. Do you tend to use your phone or watch TV before bed? If yes, do you think it affects your sleep quality?

5. Consider your dream world. Have you noticed any changes in your dreams? Note down any interesting dreams you've had lately.

Remember, your journal is your private space, don't worry about making it perfect or impressive. It's all about expressing yourself honestly and openly.

☆ 6.3 IMPORTANCE OF ROUTINE

Creating a healthy daily routine can be one of the most empowering things in life, especially while undergoing something as big as puberty. It can help you stay balanced and focused, while also easing some of the changes and surprises that puberty might bring. Here's how you can build your daily routine in a way that promotes health, positivity, and growth:

★ Establish a consistent wake-up and bedtime. Sleep is extremely important during puberty, as it's when your body does most of its growing and repairing. Try to aim for at least 9 hours of sleep each night.

★ Eating balanced meals is also crucial. Make sure your diet includes all the necessary nutrients for a growing body: proteins, carbohydrates, plenty of fruits and vegetables, and a good amount of water. Try not to skip meals, even if you're not feeling hungry. Your body needs the energy to cope with all the changes it's undergoing.

★ Physical activity is a vital part of any routine. Aim to exercise for at least 30 minutes each day. It doesn't all have to be in one go, and it certainly doesn't have to be boring. Dancing, jumping rope, biking or just running around the park can all contribute to your daily quota.

★ Mental health is as important as physical health. Dedicate a portion of your day to activities like reading, drawing, playing a musical instrument or anything else that engages your mind and brings you joy.

★ Remember to practice good hygiene, especially now that your body is changing. Regular showers, brushing, and flossing your teeth, washing your hands, and taking care of your skin, hair, and nails are all important aspects of personal cleanliness.

★ Allot some quiet time for yourself. Puberty can be a roller coaster of emotions, and it's essential to tune in, understand, and respect these feelings. This should be a time where you can relax, reflect, and recharge. You could use this time to write in a journal, practice mindful meditation, or even just sit in silence.

Sometimes, creating a new routine and sticking to it can be a tough task. To make it easier, consider implementing a reward system. Rewards are a great way to motivate yourself and make the process of forming a routine more enjoyable. Don't worry, the rewards don't have to be huge or expensive. You could treat yourself to your favorite snack after a week of consistent exercise, or allow yourself an extra hour of your favorite show after maintaining a healthy eating habit. Be creative and think about what would really motivate you. Creating a visualization board is also a great way to keep your goals in sight. You could cut out pictures of things that represent your goals and what you want to achieve, and stick these on your board. Visualization is a powerful tool to keep you focused and motivated.

Monitoring progress can also be very rewarding. Creating a chart to fill in or track habits may make sticking to the routine a bit more exciting. Maybe you can color a spot for each day you stick to your routine, and once the chart is filled, celebrate your achievement. Using positive affirmations can also help encourage consistency. Affirmations are short, powerful statements that help to shift your mindset and keep you focused. You might say things like "I am strong," "I am capable," or "I am making healthy choices every day." To sum up, developing a healthy daily routine is vital during puberty, but remember that it's okay if you miss a step in your routine once in a while. What's important is consistency, so do your best to adhere to the routine as much as possible and keep going. You'll be surprised at the powerful changes a well-established, consistent routine can bring about.

As you begin to grow and change, it becomes apparent that your old routines might not cut it anymore. The way you did things when you were younger, from skin care to how you manage your time, might not suit your needs as you edge closer to becoming a teenager. One of the first things you might notice changing is your skin. As your body starts to produce more hormones, you might find that your skin is more oily than usual, which can lead to breakouts. No need to panic, though. This is a completely normal part of growing up.

-> Here's what you can do: Start incorporating a gentle, non-comedogenic cleanser into your nighttime routine. Wash off the dirt and sweat accumulated throughout the day to combat potential breakouts.

Food cravings can also be intense during this phase. You might feel an increasing desire for sweets, junk food, and sometimes, combinations of food that might seem a little absurd to adults.

-> Here's what you can do: Listen to your body, but don't let cravings dictate your diet. Balance is key. Eat protein-rich food, fruits, vegetables, and whole grains. Treat yourself occasionally - it's okay, nobody's perfect.

Another area that might require a new routine is your hygiene. Your body is changing and so too must your hygiene habits. Now is the time to start considering things like underarm deodorant and changing your undergarments more regularly.

-> Here's what you can do: Keep a personal hygiene kit handy. This could include a travel-sized deodorant, wet wipes, and an extra pair of undergarments.

Embracing these physical changes is just as important as adapting to the whirlpool of emotions that may often hit you unexpectedly. Mood swings can feel overwhelming and, sometimes, you might not even understand why you are feeling a certain way.

-> Here's what you can do: Maintaining a 'feelings journal' can be highly beneficial in understanding the pattern of your emotions. Write down what you're feeling as honestly as possible, it is only for your eyes, after all.

Time management can become more challenging as more responsibilities and activities come into your life, be it homework, household duties or extracurricular activities.

-> Here's what you can do: Start using planners or digital apps to help you manage your time more efficiently. Prioritize your tasks and be sure to allot some 'me' time as well.

Remember, change is a part of life and your growing years are as much about understanding these changes as they are about experiencing them. Welcome change with open arms and never hesitate to ask for guidance when needed. After all, everyone you know and look up to has been through this phase - they might have some helpful tips and advice for you. So, keep your mind open, your spirit strong, and march ahead with confidence in your journey to growing up.

Journal Exercise:

List down your daily routine from the moment you wake up to when you go to bed. Once you've done that, mark the activities that are routine - like brushing your teeth, showering, eating your meals, and going to school. Are there areas where you have no routine? How does that lack of structure affect your day or your emotions? How can you develop a routine to address that? After the changes you are experiencing in your body, what routines do you need to include? Remember, routines make our lives organized and less chaotic, especially during periods of great change like puberty. Write about your thoughts here.

Chapter 7

TALKING TO ADULTS

☆ 7.1 CONVERSATIONS WITH PARENTS

So, you have a bunch of questions bouncing around your head about puberty, and you think it's high time you had a good old chat with your parents. This can seem nerve-wracking, but don't worry, it's completely normal. Here are some helpful strategies to make starting those conversations a little bit easier. Firstly, choose the right time and place. This might be during a quiet afternoon at home, during a car ride, or even on a walk. Ideally, it should be a time when you won't be interrupted and both you and your parent are relaxed.

Next, think about what you want to ask or talk about beforehand. Writing your questions or concerns down on paper can help you organize your thoughts. It's completely okay to bring your notes to the conversation; it will show your parents that you are serious about the matter. The most important thing is to be honest about how you feel. If you're embarrassed or uncomfortable, tell your parent. They were young once too and they'll understand. If you're not sure how to start the conversation, you could say something like, "I've been thinking about some changes that are happening, and I have some questions." Remember, there is no such thing as a silly question. If something is bothering you or you're not clear on something, ask away. Understanding your body and what's happening to it is important, and your parents are there to help guide you. Keep in mind these conversations don't have to happen all at once. It's okay to have lots of little chats rather than one big 'puberty talk.' It might be less overwhelming that way. If at first a discussion doesn't go as planned, don't be disheartened. It might take a little time for your parents to adjust to the fact that you're growing up. Give them some time and try again later.

When you look in the mirror, it's natural to notice that you're not the same person you were a couple of years ago or even a few months ago. You've grown taller, developed new curves, and maybe even started to wear a bra. On the inside, you also have a lot of changes. This can be exciting and frightening at the same time, and it's okay to feel overwhelmed. But you're not alone on this journey. Your parents, aunts, uncles, older siblings, and friends have been through similar experiences. Talking about your feelings, doubts, and concerns with your parents can be tough, especially because you may feel they won't "get" you. But remember, they were your age once and went through similar changes. Not only can they provide advice and comfort, but they can also ease your worries and confusion about what's happening to you. This doesn't mean they'll have all the answers, but they can offer their experience and perspective.

Here's what helps when trying to bridge the gap with your parents:

★ Open up: Parents are a great source of guidance and support. It may seem like they won't understand what you're going through, but more often than not, they will. Share what you're feeling, and remember that it's okay to not understand everything that's happening.

★ Be patient: Remember that it's okay if your parents don't immediately understand how you're feeling. Give them some time to process the information, and try to approach discussions calmly and patiently.

★ Avoid blaming and accusations: When you're upset, it's easy to blame others for your feelings. Try to share your feelings without blaming or accusing your parents. Instead, focus on expressing how you feel.

Physical changes are just one aspect of puberty - your emotions can fluctuate too. One minute, you may feel like you're on top of the world, and the next, you might feel like nobody understands you. These feelings can sometimes make it seem like you and your parents are on different pages. The key is to communicate. When your emotions are running high, take a deep breath and tell them how you're feeling. Learning to understand your parents' perspective can help to build better communication and strengthen your relationship during this transitional phase. Remember, they care about you and want to help you navigate these changes as smoothly as possible. Also, keep in mind that everyone's experience with puberty is different, so what worked for your parents might not work for you - and that's okay. This is your individual journey, and it's all about finding what makes you comfortable and puts your mind at ease.

Journal Exercise:

1. Reflect on your feelings and thoughts on discussing puberty with your parents. What do you feel comfortable talking about? What feels uncomfortable, and why might that be?

2. Write down two questions you'd like to ask your parents about puberty. They can be about physical changes, emotional experiences, or other aspects that interest or worry you.

3. Now, imagine the reactions or responses you think your parents might have to these questions. How does their imagined response make you feel?

4. Are you afraid of their reactions, if so why? Are there ways you could ask these questions where you'd feel safer or more comfortable?

5. Finally, write down one step you could take towards having a conversation with your parents about puberty during the upcoming week. How will you ensure you feel prepared and comfortable for this talk?

☆ 7.2 TALKING TO TEACHERS AND COUNSELORS

We often think of changes during this period of time as mostly physical, but there are also shifts that occur within the realm of our relationships, behavior, and emotions. One such shift may take the form of growing closer to your teachers and counselors. Let's discuss this aspect in detail. Just as you are growing and changing, your relationship with your teachers and counselors at school are likely to evolve as well. As we embark on this journey of understanding and navigating these changes, here are some strategies and tips:

★ Listening is the Key: Always remember that your teachers and counselors are there to support you. When you engage them in conversation, try to actively listen to their advice. This will not only show them that you respect their input, but also allow you to fully understand their perspective.

★ Be Open about Your Feelings: Expressing your feelings can be a daunting task, especially when it's about something so personal as puberty. However, sharing how you feel with your teachers or counselors can help them guide you better.

★ Plan Your Conversation: Sometimes it can be hard to put your thoughts into words. It's a good idea to jot down the main points you would like to discuss. This way, you can ensure you won't forget to mention anything important.

★ Be Respectful: Even if you may not agree with a point your teacher or counselor makes, remember to always show respect. A difference of opinion doesn't necessarily mean that one person is wrong and another is right.

★ Don't Hesitate to Ask Questions: If there's something you don't understand or if you need more information, feel free to ask. Your teachers and counselors are there to help you.

Building strong and trusting relationships with your teachers and counselors can truly make your transition to adulthood smoother. So, next time you find yourself overwhelmed by the changes you're going through, remember there are caring adults right there at your school, eager to listen and offer the guidance you need.

SITUATION OR CONCERN	WHAT TO SAY	POSSIBLE OUTCOMES
Bullying at school	I am being harassed by some students.	The teacher takes immediate action
Difficulty in understanding a subject	I'm struggling to understand this topic.	Extra help or tutoring is offered
Feeling physically unwell	I'm not feeling well today.	You're sent to the school nurse

SITUATION OR CONCERN	WHAT TO SAY	POSSIBLE OUTCOMES
Worried about a friend's behavior	I'm concerned about my friend's well-being.	Counselor offers to talk to your friend
Struggling with school-workload	I'm overwhelmed with the amount of work.	Teachers provide advice on managing your time
Issues at home affecting school	I'm having trouble concentrating due to issues at home.	Referral to a school counselor and parental involvement

Journal Exercise:

Reflect on a time when you felt like you needed to talk to a teacher or a counselor about something that was bothering you. Who was this person, why did you choose them, and what was the situation? If you haven't had this experience yet, imagine a scenario where you might need to reach out for help. Write a short dialogue of what you would say to them and what you would hope their response would be. Also, write down how the conversation with your teacher or counselor (real or imagined) affected or could affect your feelings about the situation.

☆ 7.3 ASKING FOR HELP

There's a lot happening as we grow up, changes are taking place almost daily, and that can sometimes make things a tad puzzling. It's perfectly normal and okay not to have all the answers, and that's when seeking help comes in. Here's the exciting part there's plenty of avenues open to you when you have questions or need to talk about what's happening. Your parents or guardians are your number one go-to persons. They have been where you are now and understand what you're going through. They want to see you happy, confident, and knowledgeable about these changes. So, whether it's about periods, emotions, or physical changes, feel free to approach them. They have the wisdom to guide, advise, or even just give you a listening ear. Teachers and counselors at school are also a valuable resource. They are trained to handle many of the problems young people face, and they are available to listen and help you find solutions. Don't be nervous or embarrassed - they've had hundreds of students asking them all sorts of questions. Doctors and healthcare professionals are equipped to explain all about puberty, your body, and your health. They are committed to keeping your information confidential. So regardless of the question, they're ready to help.

Friends going through the same stage of life can be a source of immediate understanding and sympathy. Sharing your experiences and worries with trusted friends not only eases your concern but can also strengthen your bond. However, remember that your friends are also learning, so what they think might not be always accurate. Books and approved websites can be your silent friend. They offer heaps of information about puberty, the changes, and how to handle them. Researching and reading on your own can enhance your knowledge and give you more control over your body and feelings.

Here is how you can ask for help:

1. Prepare: Write your questions down if that makes you feel more prepared. It may feel a little less overwhelming and helps to make sure you don't forget anything.

2. Choose the right time: Find a quiet, relaxed moment to bring up your questions or concerns. It could be after dinner, during a car ride, or during a leisurely walk.

3. Be honest: Remember, there's no need to feel ashamed or embarrassed. Puberty is a natural process that happens to everyone.

4. Listen carefully: When you ask for help, be sure to listen to the advice or answers you are given.

5. Say thank you: Always thank the person helping you. They've taken time to assist you, and a little appreciation goes a long way.

No question is too silly or unimportant. If something is bothering you or making you curious, it's often a good idea to ask about it.

Journal Exercise:

Write down three feelings you experience when considering asking for help from someone, especially regarding the changes you're experiencing. Explain why you feel this way.

List three people you could ask for help and write why you chose them.

Choose one of these individuals and write down what you would say to ask for their help. This could be a real conversation or just a hypothetical situation.

Think about a time when you did ask for help - how did you feel afterwards? Record what happened and any emotions you experienced.

Lastly, imagine your best friend has the same worries about asking for help as you do. Write a short letter offering her advice based on your reflections and experience.

Chapter 8

FREQUENTLY ASKED QUESTIONS

☆ 8.1 COMMON QUESTIONS AND CONCERNS

Every girl's journey into puberty is unique, filled with many questions, wild emotions, puzzling changes, and more than a sprinkle of wonder. Let's start by tackling some of the most common questions and worries at this stage of life.

Why am I feeling so emotional lately?

Feeling like you're on an emotional roller coaster is perfectly normal during puberty. Your body is brimming with newfound hormones that can cause mood swings. One minute you might be laughing, the next you might feel like sobbing. Don't worry, these whirlwind emotions will stabilize as you get used to these new hormones.

Is it normal to experience body odor?

Yes, it is. As you start puberty, your sweat glands start to work more, especially under your arms. This sweat can sometimes smell more than it used to, leading to body odor. Regularly washing and using a mild deodorant can help you manage this.

Why are my friends growing faster than me?

Puberty is like a marathon, not a sprint. Everyone starts and finishes at their pace, and that's perfectly OK. Some of your friends might start developing breasts or get their periods earlier than you. Rest assured, your body is catching up on its own time.

Do I have to shave my legs and underarms?

Shaving is a personal choice and by no means a necessity. Some girls feel more comfortable and confident after shaving, while others prefer not to. There is no right or wrong decision.

Why is my chest hurting sometimes?

As your breasts begin to develop, it's perfectly normal to feel a little soreness or tenderness. It can be pretty uncomfortable, but this is just a sign that your body is growing and changing.

When will I start my period?

Most girls get their first period between 10-15 years old, but it can start earlier or later than this. Some clues that your period may be starting soon include breast development, pubic hair growth, and a growth spurt.

How can I deal with acne?

It's common to get acne during puberty because of changing hormones. To help keep acne at bay, wash your face twice a day with mild soap and warm water, avoid touching your face with unwashed hands, and resist the urge to squeeze pimples, which can make them worse.

Questions are your best friends in times of change. No worry is too small or silly. This time of transition is unique to everyone, so it's entirely normal if you experience things not mentioned here or if you're feeling anxious or excited by the changes. You are growing beautifully, and these changes are significant steps towards becoming the wonderful, confident young woman you are meant to be.

☆ 8.2 MYTHS AND MISCONCEPTIONS

Sometimes, you might hear things about growing up that, honestly, can sound pretty fantastical or even scary. But it's crucial to remember that not everything you hear or read is accurate, especially when it comes to changes during puberty. Let's break down some of the most common myths and misconceptions about puberty you may have come across to help you understand the truth better.

1. It's been said that girls who get their periods are not children anymore. This couldn't be further from the truth! Getting a period signifies that your body is maturing physically, but it does not mean you are suddenly an adult mentally or emotionally. Yes, you are growing up, but you're still a kid, and you are allowed and encouraged to enjoy your childhood.

2. Another common myth is that girls need to start wearing a bra once they hit puberty. The truth is that wearing a bra is a personal choice. Some girls find bras comfortable or need them for support during physical activities. Others feel better without them. Do what feels right for you.

3. You might also have heard that only girls with large breasts will have soreness during puberty. This, too, is not

true. Soreness is a part of the growth and has nothing to do with the size of your breasts.

4. Something else commonly believed is that girls gain weight during puberty because they're „eating too much." This is very misleading. During puberty, it's normal and necessary for your body to gain weight, no matter what or how much you eat. Your body is developing, and it needs the extra energy.

5. The saying that ,acne appears because you don't cleanse properly' is another myth. Acne during puberty is primarily due to hormonal changes. It's not your fault, and it doesn't mean you aren't clean. Regular cleansing can help, but if it's persistent, you may want to speak to a doctor.

6. You may also have heard that puberty starts at the same time for everyone, and if you're late, something is wrong. That's not accurate! Everyone goes through puberty on their own schedule. It's perfectly okay to be an early or late bloomer.

7. The final misconception to debunk is that you don't need to see a doctor for menstrual cramps. Severe pain during your period isn't routine, and you should let a medical professional know. There are ways to manage it, and you certainly don't need to suffer in silence.

Puberty is a unique journey for everyone. It's easy to get overwhelmed by all the stories and information floating around. The important thing is to be patient, kind, and understanding towards yourself. Don't hesitate to ask questions or find sources you trust - like doctors, parents, or teachers - if you're ever in doubt about these or other facets of growing up.

Journal Exercise:

1. Reflect on a myth or misconception about puberty you believed before reading this chapter.

2. Write it down.

3. How did this belief make you feel about puberty?

4. After reading the chapter, what facts did you learn that dispelled this myth?

5. How do you feel about puberty now?

6. Think about how you could kindly and respectfully inform a friend who still believes this myth. Practice writing the conversation down.

Chapter 9

RESOURCES AND SUPPORT

☆ 9.1 BOOKS AND WEBSITES

By now, you've ventured deep into the world of puberty, gaining insights into your changing body, evolving emotions, and the intricate maze of relationships. But there's always more to learn and explore. That's why, in this section, we're introducing you to some fantastic resources – both books and websites – that can provide further information, stories, and even a dose of entertainment!

Books to Read

I. "The Care & Keeping of You: The Body Book for Younger Girls" by Valorie Schaefer

This is an excellent starter book that covers basic body changes during puberty. It's packed with illustrations and straightforward explanations perfect for your age.

2. "It's Perfectly Normal: Changing Bodies, Growing Up, Sex, and Sexual Health" by Robie H. Harris

A more in-depth guide that includes the science of puberty and covers topics related to sex education. It's candid, easy to understand, and incredibly informative.

3. "The Feelings Book: The Care & Keeping of Your Emotions" by Dr. Lynda Madison

This one dives deep into the emotional roller-coaster that comes with puberty, providing guidance on how to handle your feelings in various situations.

4. "Stand Up for Yourself & Your Friends: Dealing with Bullies & Bossiness and Finding a Better Way" by Patti Kelley Criswell

An essential read on navigating challenging relationships and standing up against bullying.

Websites to Explore

I. GirlsHealth.gov

This site is a treasure trove of information on all things related to girls' health. It covers topics ranging from body changes to dealing with emotions and provides answers to many of the questions you might have.

2. KidsHealth.org - for Kids

Another fantastic resource packed with articles, slideshows, and quizzes about health, emotions, and life in general.

3. The Period Blog

A platform dedicated to menstruation, it offers product reviews, advice, and real-life experiences shared by other girls and young women.

4. Dove Self-Esteem Project

Focused on body positivity and building self-esteem, this site offers tools, articles, and workshops to help boost your confidence.

Remember, books and websites are tools to further your understanding, but always be cautious. Not everything on the internet is accurate or helpful. It's a good idea to discuss what you read with a trusted adult, like a parent, teacher, or counselor, especially if you're unsure about something. Additionally, while books and websites are great, personal stories from people you trust can also provide insights. Talk to older siblings, cousins, or friends who've been through puberty. Their experiences, wisdom, and advice can be invaluable!

☆ 9.2 HELPLINES AND SUPPORT GROUPS

Hi there, wonderful reader! Remember that while books and websites are valuable sources of information, sometimes we might need a more immediate, human touch to help us through confusing or challenging times. Helplines and support groups can provide exactly that — a listening ear, advice from experts, or shared experiences from peers going through the same thing.

Understanding Helplines and Support Groups

Before diving into our list, it's important to understand what these resources are:

Helplines: These are usually toll-free phone numbers you can call to get advice, support, or even just someone to talk to. They're operated by trained professionals or volunteers who can listen, provide information, and guide you to appropriate resources if needed.

Support Groups: These are gatherings (either in person or online) of individuals who share common challenges or experiences. In a support group, you can share your feelings, listen to others, and get advice in a safe and supportive environment.

Helplines to Consider:

1. Girls' Crisis Helpline

A helpline dedicated to helping girls going through difficult situations. Whether it's confusion about puberty, problems at school, or struggles at home, they're there to help.

2. National Eating Disorders Association (NEDA) Helpline

If you or someone you know is struggling with body image or eating concerns, NEDA provides support, resources, and treatment options.

3. Teen Line

Run by teens for teens, this helpline is perfect for when you just need someone your age to talk to. They're trained to help with a variety of issues, from stress and relationship problems to more severe challenges.

4. The Trevor Project

For LGBTQ+ youth who need someone to talk to, The Trevor Project offers a helpline, text, and chat services.

Support Groups to Explore

I. Girl Scouts

While it's not a traditional support group, Girl Scouts offers an environment where you can make friends, learn new skills, and discuss challenges with trusted adults and peers.

2. School Counseling Groups

Many schools offer group counseling sessions on topics like self-esteem, stress management, and more. Check with your school counselor for information.

3. Local Community Centers

Often, community centers or local organizations host group sessions for teens and pre-teens on topics like puberty, body image, and mental health.

4. Online Forums

Sites like "Girl Zone" and others offer a space for girls to chat, share experiences, and get advice in a moderated environment.

Always remember to prioritize safety. If attending in-person groups, always let someone you trust know where you're going. If exploring online forums, avoid sharing personal information and remember that while many people are well-intentioned, not everyone has your best interests at heart. Always cross-check advice with trusted adults. Life during puberty can sometimes feel like a roller coaster, with high highs and low lows. Know that you're never truly alone on this ride. There are countless resources, both human and digital, available to guide, support, and uplift you. Embrace them, lean on them, and remember, every challenge faced is a step closer to the amazing young woman you're becoming.

CONCLUSION

☆ 10.1 YOU'RE NOT ALONE: THIS IS JUST THE BEGINNING

In these exciting times of growth and change, remember that you're not alone. You might feel that what's happening to your body, mind, and feelings is yours to bear alone. But the fact is, every single girl all around the world goes through these changes, just like you. Here are some comforting thoughts:

1. It's not a race. You might notice some girls around you developing faster or slower than you; this is completely normal. Each one of us has our unique timeline for development. Embrace yourself as you are.

2. It's okay to ask questions. There's no such thing as silly questions when it comes to understanding what's happening to your body. Reach out to trusted adults, like your parents, teacher, or doctor who can offer helpful advice.

3. You're in good company. Remember, each one of your friends will face their unique challenges and changes during puberty. So, don't feel shy about sharing your experiences with them and reassuring each other.

4. Feelings of fear or confusion are natural. You are experiencing a lot of firsts right now. Remember, it's normal to feel nervous or unsure about these changes, but they are an important part of growing up.

5. Self-love is critical. It's crucial to love and respect your body, even when you might feel like you don't understand it. Remember, your body is doing exactly what it's

supposed to do - helping you to grow into a mature and healthy person!

6. You do not always have to „fit in". Everyone's body shape, size, and color are different, and these may change during puberty too. Embrace your body for what it is. Understand that everyone is different and that it's okay if you do not look exactly like your friends, celebrities, or anyone else.

7. Staying healthy is important. Make sure you are eating good food, exercising regularly, and getting enough sleep. This will not only help you feel better physically but also help you cope with the emotional changes during puberty.

So, always remember, you're not alone. Every girl, no matter where she comes from, eventually goes through the same transformations. It's not always a smooth ride, but with patience, knowledge, and understanding, it can be a very empowering phase of your life.

Journal Exercise:

1. Write down three things you learned from this book that you didn't know before.

2. How has your perspective about puberty changed after reading this book?

3. What is the most comforting thing you learned from the ‚You're Not Alone' section and why?

4. Are there any feelings or thoughts that you still find confusing or scary? Write them down.

5. Who are the people in your life you can talk to about your body and emotions? List three of them and a question you would feel comfortable asking each one about puberty.

6. Finally, make a pledge to yourself: Write down three things you will do to take care of your changing body, mind, and emotions.

Remember, you are not alone, and this is just the beginning of a beautiful journey of growing up.

☆ 10.2 FINAL THOUGHTS

As we come to the end of our journey together, I want to share some final thoughts with you.

The next few years will bring plenty of changes, and each one is a step toward turning into a remarkable young woman. No two paths to womanhood are exactly the same so remember, whatever happens and whenever it happens is just right for you. Body changes can feel strange or even uncomfortable. All the new things you're experiencing—like those tricky growth spurts, shape-shifting, and yes, even acne—are all parts of the package of becoming a teenager.

It's perfectly normal to:

1. Be excited one day about your changing body and skeptical the next.

2. Have a zillion questions, even if you're too shy or unsure to ask them.

3. Feel drawn to spending more time with friends and less time with your family.

4. Experience intense emotions that can swing from one extreme to another.

5. Feel self-conscious about how you look, act, or talk.

Remember, each and everyone go through these changes. You aren't alone! Don't let anyone or anything rush you into growing up. It's important to embrace each stage and go at your own speed. Some girls develop quickly, while others take a little longer, yet we all become fabulous young women in the end. Try not to compare yourself to others—not to your friends, siblings, or especially anyone you see on TV or in magazines. Your journey is uniquely yours, and you can't follow the same road as anyone else. You're special, and the changes you're experiencing are shaping you into an astounding individual. Keeping communication open with safe adults can also reduce fear and confusion. Chat with your folks, a family member, or a trusted teacher if you have concerns. If you're unsure about something—ask. There's no such thing as a silly question! Remember that the emotional changes you're going through are just as significant, if not more so, than the physical ones. You're growing emotionally and mentally, not just physically. Write down your thoughts and feelings, chat with a trusted friend, or create art to express yourself.

Above all, take good care of yourself! Eating well, getting enough sleep, and being active can all help you feel good. Growing up is an adventure and like all quests, there might be a few bumps along the way, but they'll make you stronger. Learn from them and keep going! Keep in mind, you're not alone, there's a whole army of girls who are facing the same changes as you. Take heart, dear one. You're on an incredible journey, and each step, no matter how big or small, is bringing you closer to becoming the fine young woman you're destined to be.

DISCLAIMER

The Ultimate Girls' Guide to Puberty is intended to provide helpful information and guidance to girls between the ages of 8 and 12 as they navigate the physical, emotional, and mental changes that come with puberty. However, it is essential to keep the following points in mind:

1. Consult with a Healthcare Professional: The information provided in this book is for educational purposes only and should not be considered a substitute for professional medical advice, diagnosis, or treatment. If you have specific health concerns or questions about puberty-related issues, please consult with a qualified healthcare provider.

2. Individual Experiences Vary: Puberty is a unique and individual experience for each person. The book provides general information about what to expect during this stage of life, but not all girls will experience the same changes at the same time or in the same way. Your personal journey through puberty may differ from what is described in this book.

3. Parental or Guardian Involvement: We strongly recommend that parents or guardians read this book alongside their child and engage in open and supportive discussions about puberty. This will allow for a more comprehensive understanding of the topic and create a safe space for questions and concerns.

4. Sensitive Content: Puberty is a topic that can be sensitive and personal. While this book aims to provide age-appropriate information, some individuals may find certain content uncomfortable or challenging to discuss. We encourage readers to seek guidance and support from trusted adults when needed.

5. Updated Information: The content in this book is accurate however, medical and scientific knowledge can evolve over time. It is essential to stay updated on the latest information and research related to puberty and adolescent health.

6. Respect for Privacy: Puberty can be a private and personal matter. It's important to respect your own privacy and the privacy of others. The book emphasizes the importance of boundaries and consent.

7. Positive Body Image: Promoting a positive body image and self-esteem is crucial during puberty. This book encourages self-acceptance and self-care while discouraging comparisons to others.

8. Legal Disclaimer: The authors, publishers, and distributors of this book are not responsible for any consequences or outcomes resulting from the use or interpretation of the information contained in this book.

In conclusion, The Ultimate Girls' Guide to Puberty is intended to be a helpful resource for girls and their families as they navigate the journey of puberty. It is not a replacement for professional advice or individualized healthcare. We hope this book serves as a valuable starting point for discussions and understanding during this important stage of life.

Made in United States
Troutdale, OR
11/15/2023

14265522R00083